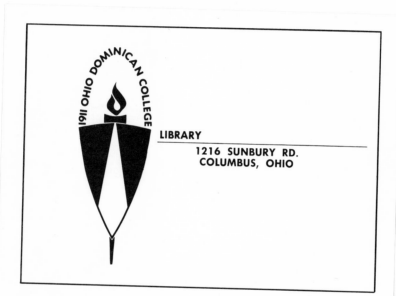

Landscape and Inscape

Vision and Inspiration in Hopkins's Poetry

Landscape
and Inscape

Vision and Inspiration in Hopkins's Poetry

Text by Peter Milward SJ
Photography by Raymond V. Schoder SJ

William B. Eerdmans Publishing Company
Grand Rapids Michigan

Published in Great Britain by
Elek Books Ltd.

Published in the U.S.A. by
William B. Eerdmans Publishing Company

Library of Congress Cataloging in Publication Data

Milward, Peter.
    Landscape and Inscape.

    1. Hopkins, Gerard Manley, 1844-1889—Criticism
and interpretation.   I. Hopkins, Gerard Manley,
1844-1889.   II. Schoder, Raymond V., 1916-
III. Title.
PR4803.H44Z719   821'.8   75-9626
ISBN 0-8028-3460-4

Printed in Great Britain

ACKNOWLEDGMENTS

The author and publishers would like to thank the English Province of the Society of
Jesus for their permission to reproduce poetry, drawings and prose writings by Gerard
Manley Hopkins. They also gratefully acknowledge the cooperation of the Oxford
University Press from whose fourth edition of *The Poems of Gerard Manley Hopkins*
(edited by W H Gardner and N H MacKenzie and published by arrangement with the
Society of Jesus) the texts of the poems are drawn; of Mr Handley-Derry and The
Humanities Research Center, University of Texas, who have given permission for the
reproduction of drawings by Hopkins in their possession; of the *Illustrated London News;*
and of all the individuals and institutions who helped towards the compilation of this
book.

Contents

List of Plates

Colour

falls of Inversnaid – The beadbonny ash, or rowantree – The groins
of the braes – Heathpacks and gorse on the braes – Rowan and
flitches of fern at the top of the burn – Yellow hornlight over St
Beuno's – The same with hollow hoarlight – Early draft manuscript
of *Spelt from Sibyl's Leaves* in GMH's Dublin notebook – An evening
sky – Beakleaved boughs against the bleak light – Portrait of a
brother and sister – Monasterevan House – Burling barrow brown near
Monasterevan – The Dry Dene of Holywell – Upper garden and
Anglican church of Holywell – Statue of St Winefred above the well
at Holywell – St Winefred's Well – The Kentish Knock – Mount
St Mary's, Derbyshire – Ventnor and Boniface Down, Isle of Wight
– Carisbrooke Castle – Appledurcombe Manor – Appledurcombe
Farm – Society of Jesus plot in Glasnevin cemetery – Memorial
window to Hopkins at St Bartholomew's, Haslemere, with detail.

Black and white

Between pages 112 and 113
The wreck of the 'Deutschland' as it appeared in the *Illustrated
London News* (18 December 1875) – The rescue of the survivors by a
Harwich steam tug – HMS 'Eurydice' struck by a squall (*Illustrated
London News*, 6 April 1878) – HMS 'Eurydice' as last seen by one of
the survivors

Facing page 128
Sketch of a tree by GMH, 1863 – Drawing of hedgerow leaves and
branches by GMH, 1863 – Drawing 'At the Baths of Rosenlaui' by
GMH, 1868 – GMH photographed with the community at Clongowes
in 1884 or 1885 – The inscription on the cross in the Jesuit plot at
Glasnevin, Ireland.

Foreword

A deep interest in the remarkable poetry of Gerard Manley Hopkins led me, some twenty-five years ago, to seek out and photograph the places in which he lived and wrote, as well as many of the particular things which he so strikingly described.

I have often lectured for college groups with some of the resultant colour transparencies in order to convey a more specific understanding of Hopkins's context and poetic skill. This has, in a sense, amounted to a new kind of approach to literature—showing the actual object or scene which Hopkins observed so sensitively, and comparing this with his description of it. The effect on an audience is wonder—delighted admiration both for his extraordinary descriptive power, often expressed with brilliant originality, and for his creative ingenuity in going beyond the objective reality into a world of his own insight and making. Few poets are his equal in making language really stand for what is experienced and observed. The best way to appreciate this is to see Hopkins the poet in action on the world around him. That is the special concern and contribution of this book.

Having been for too many years prevented by other enterprises from putting this photographic material at the disposal of a wider audience, I am pleased that it is now being used by a skilful interpreter of Hopkins's mind and art. Father Peter Milward's competence and sensitivity in elucidating Hopkins's poetry are widely esteemed in Japan as well as in England and America.

I hope that our collaboration will bring many others to share the high joy which Hopkins himself found in encountering and recognizing the beauty and mystery of God's wonder-charged world and his 'fine delight' in capturing it in such uniquely effective language—'the achieve of, the mastery of the thing!' It 'fans fresh our wits with wonder'.

Raymond V. Schoder SJ
Loyola University, Chicago, 1974

Author's Preface

Few poems in the English language more readily bear or more fully repay an exact and searching scrutiny than those of Gerard Manley Hopkins. They are so charged with ambiguity, implication, and association of various kinds that no one can say he has ever exhausted the meaning of any one poem. Then they are so rich in references to other poems and prose writings both of the poet himself and of his contemporaries and predecessors, not to mention the classics of the past, both sacred and secular. Few poets have more amply fulfilled Keats's requirement that every rift in a poem should be loaded with ore—except that Hopkins has loaded his with gold.

Some years ago I endeavoured to supply the need of a detailed commentary on his poems with two books which I published in Japan for the benefit of my students at Sophia University, Tokyo. They were *A Commentary on G. M. Hopkins' 'The Wreck of the Deutschland'* (Hokuseido, 1968), and *A Commentary on the Sonnets of G. M. Hopkins* (Hokuseido, 1969). These books came to the attention of a fellow Jesuit in America, Father Raymond V. Schoder, and he suggested I put them together with whatever additions might be necessary for a complete commentary on Hopkins's poems. To this commentary he proposed to contribute his fine collection of photographs illustrating the poems from the places where they were actually composed. This seemed a splendid idea; but it was some time before I could act on it, owing to the problem of communication between Japan and America or England. Meanwhile, two fairly comprehensive commentaries on Hopkins had come out, one by Donald McChesney in England and the other by Paul Mariani in America.

Last year, however, while passing through America to England on a sabbatical leave, I took the opportunity to visit Father Schoder at Loyola University, Chicago, in order to examine his slide collection and to discuss the future of our project. We were both desirous of going through with it, partly because the existing commentaries, though comprehensive, were still not exhaustive, and partly because neither they nor other books on Hopkins provided pictorial illustrations on the subject–matter of his poems. Here was a considerable gap in Hopkins criticism which we as his fellow Jesuits felt reasonably competent to fill. Father Schoder had spent the best part of a year in England, living mainly at St Beuno's College, and visiting other houses in which Hopkins had lived, with the aim of taking as many photographs as possible of the places and scenes which inspired the poems. As for myself, as an English Jesuit I have at one time or another lived in or visited most of the houses with which Hopkins was familiar, especially St Beuno's, where I spent the first three years of my religious life. We have both been through much the same spiritual and intellectual formation as Hopkins, and through fam–iliarity with his writings have come to see things more or less with his eyes and mind, as well as his spirit.

After viewing all the transparencies in Father Schoder's collection, I selected those I considered directly illustrative of the poems and con–ducive to the kind of book I had in mind. Later, when I could study them more at leisure, I found they conveniently fell into groups of four or five round particular passages or stanzas of certain poems, and I considered I could use these groups as nuclei for the discussion of characteristic themes or insights of the poet, while going on to give a fairly exhaustive commentary on the poem or passage in question. There is thus something selective, or anthological, rather than comprehensive about this commentary (for such it still remains in essence). It concen–trates on those poems of which I had photographs available from Father Schoder's collection, and treats them as representative of the rest, though they differ from many others in lending themselves more readily to photographic illustration. In each chapter I have aimed at giving a careful analysis of the particular poem I have chosen in the light both of Hopkins's other writings and of his general view of life, regarding it as a basic principle of criticism to interpret his poems according to his own categories of thought and imagination.

Such a plan might seem to make for a somewhat random disposition of material; but I have endeavoured to follow a certain order, which is partly logical, partly chronological, and partly geographical. For my point of departure I have naturally taken St Beuno's College, as the place where Hopkins broke his seven years of 'elected silence' with *The Wreck of the Deutschland*. Here, too, he wrote many of his 'bright sonnets', redolent of the surrounding countryside of 'this world of Wales', such as his sonnet *In the Valley of the Elwy*. Then, following the direction of Hopkins's thought in another poem of this period, *Hurrahing in Harvest*, I turn my eyes from the earth below to the sky above in a contrast of landscape and cloudscape. This contrast continues through the next two chapters, in which I dwell on two of Hopkins's best-loved sonnets of this period, *God's Grandeur* and *Pied Beauty*. Leaving St Beuno's for the time being, I consider other poems of his (not sonnets) dealing with wild flowers, such as *The May Magnificat*, and trees, such as *Binsey Poplars*. Going farther afield, I follow the poet northwards to Loch Lomond, where the impressive Scottish scenery inspired his most detailed description of a place in *Inversnaid*. Thence I follow him across the sea to Ireland, with a chapter on *Spelt from Sibyl's Leaves*, as the first of the 'dark sonnets' and representative of the others within the compass of this volume. Ireland is also represented by the unfinished poem *On the Portrait of Two Beautiful Young People*, which leads me to reflect on the poet's response to beauty not only in nature, but also in man. Turning now to the dramatic element in his poems, and returning to Wales (and going backwards in time), I discuss his unfinished drama on the story of St Winefred at Holywell. This prompts a further discussion of *The Wreck of the Deutschland* in view of the dramatic quality of its narrative, and in comparison with the other poem of shipwreck, *The Loss of the Eurydice*—this time with illustrations not only of the places involved, but also of the events as conceived by a contemporary artist in the pages of the *Illustrated London News*. Still going backwards in time, I conclude with one of Hopkins's early poems which aptly symbolizes at once his original ideal in life and his final resting-place in death at Glasnevin cemetery, Dublin. (For a full chronology, see the Appendix at the end of the book.)

Such in brief is the genesis of this book. Its publication, with a wealth of illustrations in colour, has been made possible partly by a subsidy obtained by Father Schoder from the John and Helen Condon Fund, partly by the generous co-operation of the publishers. I also owe a personal debt of thanks to Father Anthony Bischoff, of Georgetown University, to Professor Norman MacKenzie, of Queen's University in Kingston, Ontario, and to Father Alfred Thomas, secretary of the Hopkins Society in England.

Peter Milward SJ
Sophia University, Tokyo
1974

I

A Pastoral Forehead

Thou mastering me
God! giver of breath and bread;
World's strand, sway of the sea;
Lord of living and dead;
Thou hast bound bones and veins in me, fastened me flesh,
And after it almost unmade, what with dread,
Thy doing: and dost thou touch me afresh?
Over again I feel thy finger and find thee.

I did say yes
O at lightning and lashed rod;
Thou heardst me truer than tongue confess
Thy terror, O Christ, O God;
Thou knowest the walls, altar and hour and night:
The swoon of a heart that the sweep and the hurl of thee trod
Hard down with a horror of height:
And the midriff astrain with leaning of, laced with fire of stress.

The frown of his face
Before me, the hurtle of hell
Behind, where, where was a, where was a place?
I whirled out wings that spell
And fled with a fling of the heart to the heart of the Host.
My heart, but you were dovewinged, I can tell,
Carrier-witted, I am bold to boast,
To flash from the flame to the flame then, tower from the grace
to the grace.

I am soft sift
In an hourglass—at the wall
Fast, but mined with a motion, a drift,
And it crowds and it combs to the fall;

I steady as a water in a well, to a poise, to a pane,
But roped with, always, all the way down from the tall
Fells or flanks of the voel, a vein
Of the gospel proffer, a pressure, a principle, Christ's gift.

I kiss my hand
To the stars, lovely-asunder
Starlight, wafting him out of it; and
Glow, glory in thunder;
Kiss my hand to the dappled-with-damson west:
Since, tho' he is under the world's splendour and wonder,
His mystery must be instressed, stressed;
For I greet him the days I meet him, and bless when I understand.

from *The Wreck of the Deutschland*: Part I

Long before he took the gown of an English Jesuit, Gerard Manley Hopkins expressed his yearning for a life of religious contemplation in two short poems which are striking in their simplicity and the contrast they offer to the complexity of his later poems. In the first of them, written on the occasion of a nun taking the veil, the poet expresses his longing for the *Heaven-Haven* of the reward, 'Where no storms come, / Where the green swell is in the havens dumb, / And out of the swing of the sea'. In the second he dwells on *The Habit of Perfection*, alluding at once to the religious habit (involved with the veil) and the life of perfection that is expected of religious men and women; and he directs his first attention to that 'elected silence', or atmosphere of self-sacrifice and renunciation, in which he hopes to meet the Bridegroom in the marriage-feast of heaven.

The ideal expressed in these two poems Hopkins began to realize for himself on his entrance into the noviceship of the English Jesuits at Manresa House, Roehampton, in 1868. On that occasion, as he later recalled in a letter to Canon R. W. Dixon, he resolved to make a sacrifice that may be difficult for people today to understand, yet is crucial for his subsequent development as a poet and the content of his poems. This was nothing less than the sacrifice of all the poems he had written before becoming a Jesuit, and of the possibility of composing any further poems, 'as not belonging to my profession, unless it were by the wish of my superiors'. So for the next seven years, he 'wrote nothing but two or three little presentation pieces which occasion called for'—pieces such as the May verses entitled *Ad Mariam* and *Rosa Mystica*, which he

The west front of St Beuno's College, Wales
Below St Beuno's College, looking towards the Ormes
Overleaf, left Window of St Peter and St Beuno in the college chapel
Overleaf, right The college chapel

View of Maenefa from the valley (St Beuno's centre right)
Below The Vale of Clywd as seen from Maenefa
Previous page The Valley of the Elwy, near Cefn

The Rock Chapel (south of St Beuno's)
Below Close-up view of the Rock Chapel

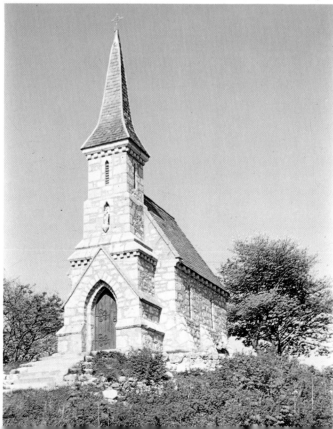

Cwm (north of St Beuno's)
Below Looking towards Moel y Parc from the Rock Chapel

may have composed during his philosophical studies at St Mary's Hall, Stonyhurst, according to the custom of Jesuit scholastics to offer verses to Our Lady during the month of May. All this time, however, he was keeping a journal, in which he recorded various experiences and observations varying between introspective self-analysis and objective description. And all this time, as he told Dixon, he had haunting his ear 'the echo of a new rhythm', which he had not as yet realized in verse.

The long maturing fruit of his sacrifice, like 'a lush-kept plush-capped sloe', came 'to flesh-burst' during his theological studies at St Beuno's College, where he was living remote from the world in circumstances similar to those envisaged in his two early poems discussed above. Then it was that, in sharp contrast to his situation 'under a roof' and 'at rest' 'away in the loveable west', he read successive accounts in *The Times* of 8 December 1875, and following days, of a sea disaster in the mouth of the Thames—the wreck of a German passenger ship called 'The Deutschland'. What particularly struck him in these accounts was the fact, mentioned in his letter to Dixon, that 'five Franciscan nuns, exiles from Germany by the Falck Laws, aboard of her were drowned'. Deeply affected by this incident, he happened to mention his feeling to the Rector of the College, who thereupon 'said that he wished someone would write a poem on the subject'. Thus it was that, together with 'the fine delight that fathers thought', the poet found himself relieved of his self-imposed obligation of silence; and so he was able to set to work, and to produce the first and greatest of his mature poems, *The Wreck of the Deutschland*.

As he read the accounts of the wreck in *The Times* that month of December, he became aware of something beyond the disaster to crew and passengers. There was evidently something in the tragedy that reminded him of the ideal expressed in those two early poems, in contrast to the way he had found this ideal realized in the peaceful surroundings of St Beuno's. For what he put at the centre of his poem—casting it as he did in the form, not of a ballad or epic narrative, but of a Pindaric Ode—was not so much the wreck of the Deutschland (though this was his title), nor the fate of the five nuns (though to them he dedicated his poem), but 'the call of the tall nun' as variously reported in *The Times* of 11 December, 'O Christ, Christ, come quickly!' and of 13 December 'My God, my God, make haste, make haste!' It was evidently this cry of hers, uttered from her heart, that appealed to the heart of the poet. Separated though they were by outward circumstances—'I was under a roof here, I was at rest, / And they the prey of the gales'—inwardly they were together in professing the same ideal or habit of perfection, and in looking to the same 'heaven-haven of the reward'. Or rather, in the distressed circumstances of the nuns the poet found himself enabled

17

to behold their common ideal more clearly than in his own restful circumstances, and so to look forward to its realization more immediately.

This is perhaps the fundamental reason why Hopkins opens his poem, not (as might have been expected) with a narrative of the wreck, leading up to the cry of the nun, but with a preliminary section of an autobiographical and theological nature. The effect of the shipwreck on him was to turn his eyes, not only outwards to the sufferings of the nuns and the 'two hundred souls' on board, but also inwards to his responsive sympathy and consequent rebirth in spirit. Here the setting of his lyric narrative is not the mouth of the Thames, but 'a pastoral forehead of Wales' where he is under the roof of St Beuno's College. Here, too, he discerns beneath the outward appearances of contrast an inward reality analogous to the 'wrecking and storm' that had overtaken those on board the Deutschland; and it is at this level of reality that the two parts of the poem come together and form a harmonious unity of meaning—in a kind of reconciliation of opposites.

The poem itself begins in the form of a prayer—or, to be more precise, of a colloquy with God consequent on the poet's meditation on the meaning of the recent shipwreck. The natural question arising out of such a disaster is why God should allow such things to happen, if he is indeed Lord and Master, controlling the boisterous winds and tides. The natural temptation for man is to rebel against the providence of God, or the seeming lack of any providence, or rather his own misconception of providence. But the more he meditates on the mystery, the more he is compelled to bow his head in confession of incomprehension. It is, no doubt, the force of this consideration which impels the poet to put himself—rather than the nuns—in the opening stanzas of his poem, in prayerful relation to God. This is a relation between 'Thou' and 'me', with the two stresses of the first line on both terms of the relation, which is characterized by the intervening verb as that of 'mastering'.

In the first half of the first stanza the poet directs his thoughts not so much to himself as to God. In view of the recent disaster, and of his continuing faith (in spite of appearances) in God's providence, he addresses God as 'giver of breath and bread'—that is, of life and the means of sustaining life—where the alliterative connection differs only by the initial 'br' from 'death and dead'. It is, in fact, as Job long before recognized, the Lord who gives and the Lord who takes away (i.21). It is he who, as the poet now repeats, is 'Lord of living and dead', with a probable echo of the opening lines of Crashaw's *Hymn to Saint Teresa*: 'Love, thou art absolute sole Lord of life and death'. His address does not, however, remain on this general level; but he continues in more particular and imaginative terms, recalling the setting of the shipwreck:

'World's strand, sway of the sea'. For if the troubles of this world are traditionally compared to a tempestuous sea—as Hopkins had previously compared them in *Heaven-Haven*—that eternity in which God has his dwelling and which is even identified with God may be called 'world's strand'. Moreover, God is not only aloof in infinite transcendence above all his creatures: he is also close to them in immanence, even when they seem to be farthest from him. As such he may be called 'sway of the sea', not only in a causative sense, as swaying or controlling the sea, but even in a formal sense, as present in the sway or movement of the sea.

Then in the second half of the stanza the poet turns from the consideration of God's mastery to himself as object. Again he recurs to the thought of Job, where he says, speaking to God: 'Thou hast clothed me with skin and flesh. Thou hast put me together with bones and sinews.' Only these words are slightly altered for the sake of alliteration and of reinforcement of sense by sound. There is significant strength in the initial 'b's of 'bound bones', rounded off as they are with nasal sounds; and this contrasts with the softness of the following 'f's in 'fastened me flesh', rounded off as they are with sibilants—with 'veins' intervening to soften the contrast. There is also a hint in the verbs, 'bound' and 'fastened', of the metaphor of ship-building which deepens the connection between the two parts of the poem. All this, however, only serves to emphasize the further contrast suggested by other words of Job: 'Thy hands have made me and fashioned me wholly round about; and dost thou thus cast me down headlong on a sudden?' Here, too, the poet chooses his words for their alliterative effect, replacing initial consonants with vowels, so as to convey a feeling by their openness of the loosening of the bonds of creation. There is also in 'unmade' an ominous echo of the 'widow-making unchilding unfathering deeps' characterized later (in stanza 13).

The poet goes on to hint at the cause of his unmaking: a feeling of dread which he specifies in the next stanza and here attributes to God's doing—according to the declaration in *Isaiah*: 'I form the light and create darkness. I make peace and create evil. I, the Lord, that *do* all these things.' (xlv.7) But, unlike Job, Hopkins asks—not 'Dost thou thus cast me down headlong?', but—'Dost thou touch me afresh?' For what he wishes to emphasize from the outset of his poem is not the dread that 'almost unmade me', but the touch of divine creativity that has given him renewed life and utterance. He therefore concludes this stanza with the monumental line that marks his entrance into a new poetry: 'Over again I feel thy finger and find thee.' The 'finger' here refers to the Holy Spirit, who is addressed in the hymn *Come, Holy Ghost* as 'finger of God's right hand', or perhaps to God's creative finger as depicted by

Michelangelo in the Sistine Chapel at Rome. The touch of this divine
finger serves to reveal God's presence once again to the inner eye of the
poet—with a possible echo of the *Canticle of Canticles*: 'I found him
whom my soul loveth' (iii.3). Thus he ends the stanza where he began,
only with the opening nominative 'Thou' changed to the concluding
accusative 'thee', and with a final stress that is all the stronger by reason
of the sprung rhythm ('fínd thée') preceding it.

In the next stanza the mention of 'dread' is more fully developed in
conjunction with imagery drawn both from the storm at the mouth of
the Thames and from the poet's own surroundings at St Beuno's. The
'dread' is here called 'terror', and described in terms of 'lightning and
lashed rod'. The poet also speaks of an experience of his at a particular
place and a particular time—'the walls, altar and hour and night'—
evidently the chapel of St Beuno's where he was meditating one night
before the Blessed Sacrament. Various conjectures have been made as to
the precise occasion of this experience; but the likeliest one is that after
reading the account of the shipwreck in *The Times*—possibly that of 11
December, which carried the first mention of the nun's cry—the poet
betook himself to the chapel that evening and experienced in his meditation a sympathetic response, both of agony and of ecstasy, to the
experience of the nuns on board the wrecked ship.

Significantly, he begins this stanza, not with the 'terror' of Christ, but
with his own impulsive reaction to this terror—a reaction in sympathetic
correspondence to that of the nun amid 'the storm's brawling'. Briefly,
his reaction is a positive 'Yes' to the apparently negative or destructive
forces of the storm; for within and behind these forces in the plural he
recognizes the singular person of Christ. His 'Yes' is thus a confession,
'truer than tongue' can tell, analogous to the confession of Saint Peter at
Caesarea Philippi, when he declared: 'Thou art the Christ, the Son of the
living God' (*Matt.* xvi.16). In contrast to this brief affirmation he
proceeds to describe the terror of his experience in terms of the storm at
the mouth of the Thames. For just as then the 'Wiry and white-fiery and
whirlwind-swivellèd snow' was spinning to the deeps, so in his own soul
he felt 'the sweep and the hurl' of God's anger treading him 'Hard down
with a horror of height', and the consequent 'swoon of a heart'. And just
as then in the case of the ship 'The breakers rolled on her beam with
ruinous shock', so in his own case he felt his 'midriff astrain with leaning
of, laced with fire of stress'. Here, too, is an echo of the *Book of Job*, when
God himself appears in the climax answering Job out of a whirlwind.

This description of his terror the poet continues into the third stanza, as
with 'The frown of his face before me' and 'the hurtle of hell Behind' he
looks frantically around for a place of refuge from imminent disaster.

Uppermost in his mind are the words of two of the Psalms: 'Whither shall I go from thy spirit? Or whither shall I flee from thy face?' (*Ps.* 138) and 'Who will give me wings like a dove, and I will fly and be at rest?' (*Ps.* 54). There is also a secondary echo of Milton's *Paradise Lost*, with reference to the fall of the angels as described by Raphael in Book VI:

> The monstrous sight
> Strook them with terror backward; but far worse
> Urged them behind: Headlong themselves they threw
> Down from the verge of Heaven; eternal wrath
> Burnt after them to the bottomless pit.

But again—as in 'almost unmade' of stanza 1—this is all abruptly contrasted by the poet's bold decision, in implementation of his 'Yes', to seek refuge with an impulsive 'fling of the heart' in 'the heart of the Host'—that is to say, in the heart of Christ present under the form of a white Host in the tabernacle before him. Thus he realizes the truth of Newman's motto: '*Cor ad cor loquitur*'.

The whole imagery of this second half of the third stanza is interestingly concentrated on wings—from the implication of Psalm 54 in the insistent question of the first half: 'Where, where was a, where was a place?' On that occasion, or 'that spell' (which may variously mean that time, or that word, or that enchantment), he 'whirled out wings'—suddenly reared or sprouted wings in his heart, as we find later on in *Hurrahing in Harvest:* 'The heart rears wings . . . / And hurls for him.' His wings are like those of a dove, as in Psalm 54; and as such he seeks rest not anywhere, but, like the dove (in *Cant.* ii.10) 'in the clefts of the rock, in the hollow places of the wall', that is, according to the traditional interpretation, in the five wounds of Christ. Moreover, in the spirit of Psalm 41, the poet speaks to his own heart, congratulating himself on having grown wings with the wit of a carrier or homing pigeon. This is also his idea in *The Handsome Heart*, where he expresses his admiration of the heart of man,

> which, like carriers let fly—
> Doff darkness, homing nature knows the rest—
> To its own fine function, wild and self-instressed,
> Falls light as ten years long taught how to and why.

Then in his flight he flashes 'from the flame to the flame'—from the flame of God's anger and the torments of hell to the higher flame of God's love and the happiness of heaven. He also towers, like a falcon (*cf. Macbeth* 11.4), 'from the grace to the grace'—from the grace of fear of God's punishments to the higher grace of love of God's goodness, in the meaning of Saint John: 'And of his fulness we all have received; and grace for grace' (i.16).

Out of this experience of divine terror and his own human response there comes in stanza 4 a new feeling of peace and harmony, presented in terms of his immediate surroundings. First, he compares his natural life to 'an hourglass' that is fixed to 'the wall / Fast'—such as was formerly used for measuring time. Or rather, he compares his life to the 'soft sift' of sand in an hourglass, which seems firm enough at its wall of glass, but at its centre is 'mined with a motion' as the sand in the upper half steadily pours down into the lower half—'And it crowds and it combs to the fall'. Here, too, is implied a further image of a boat drawn up on a sandy shore and attached by a rope to the sea wall, yet 'mined with a motion' as the waves break around it and draw the sand from beneath its keel. Of these two images the former is predominant, with the explicit mention of 'an hourglass', whereas the latter is implicit in the description following the dash. In either case there is a strong rhythmic emphasis on 'the fall', suggestive both of the poet's own sinking feeling at heart and of the further theological association with the original sin of Adam, or Fall of Man, which prevails over all natural life.

On the other hand, the second comparison in the second half of the stanza is to 'water in a well', which is maintained in constant equilibrium not by natural power, but by 'Christ's gift' of sanctifying grace. Now in contrast to the 'soft sift / In an hourglass', the poet thinks of himself in terms of 'a water in a well', which is kept 'to a poise, to a pane'. Here the very repetition of the indefinite article, even at the expense of English grammar, the consequent regularity of the metre, in a series of anapaests ('aŝ ă wáter iñ ă well, tŏ ă póise, tŏ ă páne'), and the alliterative balance of 'water' and 'well', 'poise' and 'pane', all serve to reinforce his thought. This equilibrium, he goes on to emphasize, is not self-sufficient, but derived from the continual supply of water (a traditional image of divine grace) coming down from above, or 'roping'—as Hopkins often describes the downward flow of a mountain stream in his Journal.

Here, too, the poet again has recourse to the imagery of his hilly surroundings at St Beuno's—in conjunction with his memory of past surroundings at Stonyhurst. For the hills from which the water descends to replenish his well are variously termed 'tall / Fells', as in north-west England (e.g. Longridge Fell near Stonyhurst), and 'flanks of the voel', as in one of the hills to the north of St Beuno's (named 'the Voel'). In plainer language, the water descending from above is 'a vein / Of the gospel proffer', brought by Christ to men on earth, even as his descent to hell is described later as 'A vein for the visiting of the . . . penitent spirits' (stanza 33). It is the divine gift, or principle of life, which Christ offers us in the Gospel and presses us to accept to the full extent of his providential mastery over creation.

In this consideration of all he has and is, both in fallen human nature and by divine grace, the poet proceeds in stanza 5 to express his fine delight and impulsive gratitude to God. Like a human lover, he kisses his hand to the stars at night, with their 'lovely-asunder / Starlight', not for what he sees in them, but for what they waft out of them ever so gently—namely, the feeling of God's presence. The same impulse he expresses later, with even more exuberance, in *Hurrahing in Harvest*, as he discerns in the movement of the clouds 'a / Rapturous love's greeting'. Nor is it only in the gentle 'stress' of the stars, but also in the rough 'stroke' of thunder, that he feels an inner glow and a sensation of glory—like the author of Psalm 28: 'The voice of the Lord is upon the waters: the God of majesty hath thundered.' From his elevated position at St Beuno's, looking out over the wide Vale of Clwyd, he had ample opportunity to observe the varying moods of the sky, both in the clear stars at night and in thunder-storms during the day. Above all, he could appreciate the beauty, not so much of sunrises in the east (as St Beuno's is situated on the western slope of 'dark Maenefa the mountain'), as of sunsets in the west on the other side of the valley. So he again kisses his hand 'to the dappled-with-damson west'—as it were counter-balancing his reference to the 'crimson-cresseted east' in the last stanza of the poem.

Finally, he touches on the heart of the mystery as he affirms God's presence 'under the world's splendour and wonder'. Similarly, in *Hurrahing in Harvest* he affirms that 'the azurous hung hills are his world-wielding shoulder'. This is a truth, he adds, which must not be taken for granted, but which must be repeatedly recognized in the mind and affirmed with the will—or, to use Hopkins's favourite term, 'in-stressed' in the mind and 'stressed' with the will. Consequently, he greets him with an affirmative 'Yes' whenever he meets him, whether in terror or in love; and he further blesses him with 'a / Rapturous love's greeting' whenever he recognizes the inner meaning of divine love in the world. This is the recognition he goes on to describe with reference first to the Life and Passion of Christ, and then to the life and passion of the five nuns on board the Deutschland. And out of each description he proceeds to draw a doxology, or hymn of praise, with which he concludes each of the two parts of his poem, justifying 'the ways of God to men', not in spite of, but by means of the disasters he sends and the sufferings he causes. For it is when he most wrings the heart that God is most revealed as Father; and it is when he has his 'dark descending' that he is most merciful.

2

This World of Wales

I remember a house where all were good
   To me, God knows, deserving no such thing:
   Comforting smell breathed at very entering,
Fetched fresh, as I suppose, off some sweet wood.
That cordial air made those kind of people a hood
   All over, as a bevy of eggs the mothering wing
   Will, or mild nights the new morsels of Spring:
Why, it seemed of course; seemed of right it should.

Lovely the woods, waters, meadows, combes, vales,
All the air things wear that build this world of Wales;
   Only the inmate does not correspond:
God, lover of souls, swaying considerate scales,
Complete thy creature dear O where it fails,
   Being mighty a master, being a father and fond.

In the Valley of the Elwy

Of his sonnets composed at St Beuno's College in the aftermath of his *Wreck of the Deutschland* there is only one in which Hopkins makes explicit reference to his Welsh surroundings. Its very title, *In the Valley of the Elwy*, points to a landscape that was never far from his eyes during his three-year sojourn at the college. The actual valley in which, or above which, this college is situated is indeed the larger Vale of Clwyd; but into the river Clwyd just below the cathedral city of St Asaph flows the smaller but lovelier river Elwy. From St Beuno's one can discern the valley through which the Elwy flows down from the mountains and foothills on the other side of the Vale of Clwyd; and one can easily reach this valley—whether at St Asaph or higher up at the caves of Cefn—on an afternoon walk. It was on one such occasion, as he was returning home from a fishing expedition by the river Elwy, that Hopkins felt inspired to compose another sonnet of this period, *Hurrahing in Harvest*.

Something about this valley, as he saw it in the spring of 1877, evidently aroused in the poet a particular memory of his past—not only by comparison, but also by contrast. Echoing the opening words of a famous poem by Thomas Hood, he begins his own poem: 'I remember a house'. What he remembers about this house—which he later identified in a letter to his friend Bridges as that of 'the Watsons of Shooter's Hill' to the east of London, and 'nothing to do with the Elwy'—is first, that 'all were good to me', and secondly, that 'comforting smell breathed at very entering'. The goodness of the Watsons to him he appreciated all the more deeply as he felt his own unworthiness—which he expresses in a somewhat banal manner in the second line: 'To me, God knows, deserving no such thing'. What he particularly remarked was the correspondence between their goodness and the fragrance of flowers at the entrance to their house, where they had been arranged in a vase so as to afford what Wordsworth calls an 'impulse from a vernal wood'.

This correspondence between the inner disposition of 'these kind people' and the 'cordial air' of their outer habitation is developed by the poet in the following quatrain in a series of metaphors and comparisons. First, the air is characterized as 'cordial', in the sense not only of hearty, as in 'a cordial welcome', but also of health-giving, as in 'a cordial tonic'. It is seen as forming over these people a kind of 'hood', suggesting the cowl of a monk in his retired cloister, which may not make the monk, but at least protects him in his religious life. Then it is further compared to 'the mothering wing' of a bird covering her 'bevy of eggs'—just as in *The May Magnificat* the 'throstle above her nested / Cluster of bugle blue eggs thin / Forms and warms the life within'. Or again, on a vaster scale, it may be likened to the 'mild nights' that foster 'the new morsels of Spring', such as the fresh 'leaves and blooms' noted on the 'glassy peartree' in the sonnet on *Spring*. In 'morsels' is contained the suggestion at once of nurslings requiring careful attention and of dainty titbits for the appetite of 'devouring Time'. Finally, as though brushing off the question 'Why?' to all these comparisons, the poet concludes that with such a house and such people the presence of 'that cordial air' was only to be expected—'of course'—as something due to them in justice—'of right' (formed by grammatical analogy with 'of course').

It seems strange that so detailed a description of a house far away in Shooter's Hill should occupy the whole octet of a sonnet entitled *In the Valley of the Elwy*. It is, in fact, only from a letter written two years after the poem that we learn from the poet that it has 'nothing to do with the

Elwy'. Without his denial it might well be taken—as his friend evidently took it—as referring to some house in the neighbourhood of the Elwy, possibly St Beuno's College. Only the opening words, 'I remember', suggest a contrast between the poet's present locality—whether at St Beuno's or in the actual valley of the Elwy—and his past memory. The point of his description is, however, to be found in the sestet that follows, with its reference not so much to the particular valley of the Elwy, as to the whole 'world of Wales'. Here again the question naturally arises why he should have chosen such a special title for this poem, whose first half refers to a house far away in London, and whose second half explicitly includes the whole world of Wales. It may have been that the idea of the poem occurred to the poet on one of his fishing expeditions to the river Elwy. It may have been that he found the 'valley of the Elwy' more poetic, both in verbal sound and in real scenery, than the 'vale of Clwyd'. It may have been that he wished to dissociate his mention of the 'inmate' of that valley from any connection with the Jesuit community at St Beuno's in the Vale of Clwyd.

Anyhow, what follows in the sestet is at once a comparison with and a contrast to the memory related in the octet of the poem. The comparison is effectively introduced by the adjective 'lovely'—a favourite word of Hopkins, who had already used it in its other adjectival form in *The Wreck of the Deutschland* to characterize his circumstances at St Beuno's 'Away in the loveable west'. Here it is placed in a predicative position so as to qualify all the nouns that follow: 'the woods, waters, meadows, combes, vales.' This is merely a list of the most general features of a landscape, with not the slightest suggestion of an inscape (or insight into the particularity of a scene). The words seem to be chosen as much for their sound as for their meaning—beginning with 'w' in 'woods' and 'waters', continuing with 'm' in 'meadows' and 'combes', and culminating in 'vales' for its echo of the title and its rhyme with 'Wales'. Only 'combes' seems at all specific, recalling as it does the name of Cwm attached to a hill on the north side of Maenefa and St Beuno's, or rather not so much the hill itself as a curve on its western slope.

This plural list of 'lovely' features is followed by the singular summation of 'all the air things wear', which is implicitly no less cordial than that which 'made those kind people a hood' in Shooter's Hill. Only here, the poet adds, the comparison ends and the contrast begins; for 'the inmate does not correspond'. And here he comes at last to the point of his poem, as he explained it to his doubting friend: 'The frame of the sonnet is a rule of three sum *wrong*, thus: As the sweet smell to these kind people, so the Welsh landscape is *NOT* to the Welsh.' What this explanation makes clear is that 'the inmate' is not the poet himself, despite his humble admission in the second line of 'deserving no such thing'; nor the Jesuit community of St Beuno's, despite the implication in the word 'inmate' of an institution; but the Welsh people in general, with a possible reference to individual Welshmen he may have met on one particular visit to the river Elwy.

It may seem strange that Hopkins should have devoted this poem to a criticism of the Welsh people, considering that only a few years before (in 1874) he had confided to his mother how 'I have always looked upon myself as half Welsh and so I warm to them'. But his real meaning may be gathered from another sonnet of this period, *The Sea and the Skylark*, in which he has a similar criticism of the Welsh town of Rhyl as being 'shallow and frail'. There he does not limit his criticism to the Welsh town, but goes on to voice his general lament over man who, though 'life's pride and cared-for crown', has by his fall into sin 'lost that cheer and charm of earth's past prime'. In other words, what he criticizes is not the Welsh as Welsh, but as human beings, the offspring of Adam, and the town of Rhyl not as Rhyl, but as a sordid industrial town whose houses resemble that 'base and brickish skirt' he complains of in Oxford. Here he speaks of the Welsh, as in *Ribblesdale* he speaks of the English in Lancashire, considering not their nation, but their fallen race; and of them he uses the general term 'inmate', instead of inhabitant, with its unfavourable connotation of a prison or mental asylum. Between them and the lovely world they inhabit he notes a lamentable lack of correspondence, quite unlike that he had admired between the 'cordial air' and the 'kind people' of Shooter's Hill.

All the same, he does not end this poem, as he ends *The Sea and the Skylark*, on this note of lamentation. Rather, he proceeds—as he further explained in his letter to Bridges—to make a petition to God as 'the author and principle of all four terms' in the rule of three sum wrong, 'to bring the sum right'. He appeals to God, not primarily as Lord and Master, but as 'lover of souls', who is not only just in weighing the worth of his creatures with 'poising palms', but also merciful out of consideration for their weakness. In other words, God is 'considerate' not only of the worth, but also of the weakness of his creatures, in apportioning praise and blame. The poet, therefore, prays God to complete his creatures, to fill up what they lack in virtue, not out of their merits which are so defective, but out of his own love which discerns something endearing even in their defects. As he comments in his later sonnet *Felix Randal*: 'This seeing the sick endears them to us.' Hence it is that he places the adjective 'dear' in a predicative position after 'thy creature' for the sake of emphasis. He thinks of man here as in *The Wreck of the Deutschland*—'thy rebel, dogged in den'—and as later in *Ribblesdale*:

> dear and dogged man—Ah, the heir
> To his own self bent so bound, so tied to his turn.

He considers that where he 'fails', where he most needs to be completed by God, is precisely in the fact, lamented in *Ribblesdale*, that otherwise he is destined through his selfish pursuit of material gain,

> To thriftless reave both our rich round world bare
> And none reck of world after.

In his final line, therefore, the poet appeals to God first to show himself 'mighty a master'— or, as he prays in *The Wreck of the Deutschland*, to 'Wring thy rebel, dogged in den, / Man's malice, with wrecking and storm'—and thereby to show himself 'a father and fond'—or, as he adds in the same stanza 9 of *The Wreck*, to appear as 'Father and fondler of heart thou hast wrung'. Thus once more, as in *The Wreck*, so in this sonnet, the poet returns to the fundamental direction of his thought, moving through the loveliness of nature and the sinfulness of man to that glory and grandeur of God which lies at the heart of his poetic inspiration as well as of his religious vocation: *Ad Majorem Dei Gloriam*—the motto of the Society of Jesus.

3
Barbarous in Beauty

Summer ends now; now, barbarous in beauty, the stooks rise
    Around; up above, what wind-walks! what lovely behaviour
    Of silk-sack clouds! has wilder, wilful-wavier
Meal-drift moulded ever and melted across skies?

I walk, I lift up, I lift up heart, eyes,
    Down all that glory in the heavens to glean our Saviour;
    And, éyes, heárt, what looks, what lips yet gave you a
Rapturous love's greeting of realer, of rounder replies?

And the azurous hung hills are his world-wielding shoulder
    Majestic—as a stallion stalwart, very-violet-sweet!—
These things, these things were here and but the beholder
    Wanting; which two when they once meet,
The heart rears wings bold and bolder
    And hurls for him, O half hurls earth for him off under his feet.

Hurrahing in Harvest

As a poet in the Romantic tradition, Hopkins is essentially enthusiastic, stirred from his inmost depths by a power of divine inspiration. This power is present in various ways in all his poems; but in none of them is it more evident than in *Hurrahing in Harvest*. This poem he composed, as he later recalled in a letter to Bridges, as 'the outcome of half an hour of extreme enthusiasm as I walked home alone one day from fishing in the Elwy'. His road on this occasion may well have been that from Trefnant to Tremeirchion, which crosses the Vale of Clwyd in a straight line, and thus allows the pedestrian to walk for a long time with head in air without fear of bumping into any obstacle. That Hopkins was fond of leaning back and looking up at the sky, one may gather from his opening line in *The Starlight Night*: 'Look at the stars! look, look up at the skies!'—itself an echo of an experience recorded in his Journal for 1874: 'As we drove home the stars came out thick: I leant back to look at them and my heart opening more than usual praised our Lord to and in whom all that beauty comes home.' Similarly, in this poem he records how he leant back and looked up at the sky while walking along a road in the daytime, and how he was filled with enthusiasm on recognizing Christ present in the beauty of the world.

There is perhaps a fleeting tone of regret in his opening words: 'Summer ends now.' Gone is the season of hope and promise, springtime, which brings 'a strain of the earth's sweet being in the beginning in Eden garden'. Gone, too, is the time for singing the medieval refrain, 'Sumer is icumen in'; for now summer is on its way out. And as evidence of its outgoing, the 'sour scythe' has been set to the fields of corn, the corn has been bound in sheaves by the reapers and stood on end in rough stooks, while the surrounding fields have been reduced to sharp stubble. Yet the falling movement of 'Summer ends now' is immediately countered by the rising movement of 'Now, barbarous in beauty, the stooks rise'. It is as though Hopkins is recalling Keats' reminder in his *Ode to Autumn* that, no less than spring, autumn has her music and her beauty. This beauty he finds first of all in the stooks ranged along the fields on either side of the road, and he characterizes it as 'barbarous'—somehow akin to the 'brute beauty' of the windhover. From one point of view such a scene is hardly to be characterized as 'barbarous', considering its homeliness and domesticity—as in a typical painting by John Constable. But it was, no doubt, the unkempt and ragged appearance of the stooks that suggested the epithet 'barbarous' to the poet's mind—as well as the surrounding stubble, resembling the bristles on a tramp's unshaven chin. He may also have adverted to the etymology of 'beard' in 'barbarous' and its connection with the bearded ears of barley projecting upwards from the sheaves. Then, too, the roughly conical formation of the stooks may have reminded him of the wigwams or tepees of American Indians.

Following the direction of their pointing, the poet now looks up at the sky himself, and thence he derives the main impulse and inspiration for his poem. It is as if 'around' serves but to raise his thoughts to 'above'; and there he discovers the heavenly origin of all the barbarous beauty around him. First, he finds in the movement of the clouds a certain wildness and wilfulness, as it were corresponding to the barbarous beauty of the stooks. But for him these are terms not of disparagement, but of praise. In the wildness of the clouds he rejoices to see a 'lovely behaviour', as of 'mannerly-hearted' children; and in their wilfulness he discerns a paradoxical combination of soft silk and rough sack, as it were a harmonious union of nature and grace. In particular, he draws attention to the wind that blows in and through the clouds, and fills him in turn with deep inspiration. As the latter move along, impelled by the force of the 'big wind', they form 'wind-walks', moving aside for the wind to pass—or rather, for him who walks on the wings of the wind. It is for him that they show their 'lovely behaviour', wantoning and gambolling like lambs in his presence, both wild and tame, wilful and submissive to his will.

The clouds are seen, however, not as distinct forms moving along, but as continually forming and reforming out of the 'meal-drift' which is their tenuous substance. It is as though, in the poet's imagination, the meal that has been ground from the harvested corn on earth has been scattered in the heavens to drift under the wind's impulse. As it is impelled along, it is forever gathering into clouds and scattering into its component parts, forever moulding and melting to the fascinated gaze of earthly beholders. The poet, too, is fascinated by all this 'cloudscape'. Yet at the same time, like the nun in *The Wreck of the Deutschland*, he has eyes for only one thing in it all, he has but 'one fetch' in him, he 'rears himself to divine ears'. With his eyes he may look up at the clouds and their 'lovely behaviour'; but in his heart he recognizes within the clouds the presence of '*Ipse*, the only one, Christ, King, Head,' and so receives from within the wind the inspiration of the 'arch and original Breath'.

Then, in the second quatrain of his sonnet, while thinking of the sky in terms of the harvested field with Christ in mind, the poet naturally recalls the story of Ruth and Booz in the Old Testament. Ruth, too, was walking down a harvested field, gleaning the corn that had fallen from the reapers' sheaves, when she met the owner of the field, Booz, and he fell in love with her. So in time she bore him a son, Obed, the father of Jesse; and it was from the root of Jesse that there blossomed the flower of our Saviour, Christ the Lord. Comparing himself, therefore, with Ruth, the poet imagines himself walking 'Down all that glory in the heavens to glean our Saviour'. Then follows the moment of delighted recognition, as when Booz rested his eyes on Ruth and fell in love with her. At first, the poet feels nothing but astonishment, as he asks himself with mingled joy and wonder, when did he ever derive from the lips or eyes of any man a more rapturous greeting than this of divine love? In his ecstasy he receives 'fair speechless messages', such as Bassanio claimed to have received from the lady Portia, coming to him as satisfying replies to his own deepest desires. They are at once 'real', as nothing else is real, and 'round', wide open and brimming over. His rapture he expresses no less in the sound than in the sense of this quatrain. First come the short, sharp phrases of 'I walk, I lift up, I lift up heart, eyes'—in a series of strong stresses, culminating in sprung rhythm. There follows an expansive release of breath, as he reaches the goal of his desire, in 'Down all that glory in the heavens to glean our Saviour'. Then in the third line the short, sharp phrases recur, as he questions his 'eyes, heart' about other looks, other lips—only to give place to yet another release in the concluding 'Rapturous love's greeting of realer, of rounder replies'.

After such a crescendo at the end of the octet, there naturally follows a lull in the opening lines of the sestet, where the poet turns his attention to a third element in the scenery: the hills he is approaching on the other side of the valley near his home. He now sees them as 'azurous hung hills'—azurous like the skies above them. Or are they the skies themselves, where they come down to the undulating horizon and (as they are described in a later sonnet) 'betweenpie mountains'? In this case, they would seem to be hung, or suspended downwards, from the vault of heaven. Then once more the poet sees the presence of Christ, this time as a heavenly Atlas wielding the world on his unseen shoulders. He, 'our passion-plunged giant risen', bears up the whole sinful world, with his feet firmly planted on celestial soil. The majesty of Christ, recognized in the skiey hills, is stressed in its two aspects: at once strong, 'as a stallion stalwart', and sweet, as a 'very violet'. Such a strange conjunction of images may well have been suggested to the poet's mind by the appearance of the hills before him. In their shape they are joined by many a saddle, suggesting a stallion; and in their colour in the late afternoon they would be turning violet, reminding him of the flower of that name.

In the finale of his poem, the poet gathers fields, skies and hills together in one comprehensive term, 'These things'—with implicit emphasis on their reality or 'thing-ness', and with repetition to convey his feeling of enthusiasm. These things, he reflects, were here before him and independently of him: their *esse* by no means depends on their *percipi* by him or anyone else. Yet, like Adam in *Paradise Lost* asking Raphael about the stars shining at night, he cannot forbear asking himself, 'For whom this glorious sight?'—when there is no beholder to enjoy it. But now he sees the answer. They have been waiting all this time, waiting for him to come and see them. Now he, the beholder, has come; and now their being and beauty is fulfilled in his act of beholding them—or rather in his act of beholding him who is at work both in 'these things' and in 'the beholder' to bring them together in one. When this happens, something extraordinary ensues. The 'heart in hiding', dull though it be and 'unteachably after evil', somehow 'whirls out wings' as of a dove or homing pigeon, and by a divine instinct 'towers from the grace to the grace'. So it is that, filled with this instinct, the poet feels an impulse to leap upwards to embrace Christ in heaven. Not only would he leap up to

Snowdon in the evening glow
Below Stooks in the Vale of Clwyd

Silk-sack clouds
Below Meal-drift moulding and melting across skies

The dappled-with-damson west
Below, left Damsons
Below, right A sprig of sloe
Overleaf A stook-field near Stonyhurst

A sky of couple-colour
Centre left A brinded sky
Centre right A brinded calf
Bottom left Finches' wings
Bottom right Rose-moles on a trout

Landscape plotted and pieced (aerial view taken near Aberdeen)
Below left Chestnut falls
Below right Gold-vermilion coals (in a fireplace at St Beuno's)

The brown brink eastward
Below Dappled sky (West Baden, USA)

heaven, he would also push, or rather 'hurl', the earth down from under his feet, spurning it as an unworthy obstacle. This image he derives from the gambolling of lambs in the springtime, as he notes in his sonnet on *Spring*: 'The racing lambs, too, have fair their fling' and in his Journal for 1871: 'It is as if it were the earth that flung them, not themselves.'

Thus in the end of his sonnet, so far from feeling regret at the thought of harvest and the end of summer, the poet is filled with an impulse to cheer his heavenly hero, and to shout 'Hurrah!' for Christ. The declining beauty of the earth in autumn serves but to fix his attention on the abiding beauty of heaven; and there, among the 'wind-walks', he comes face to face with his Saviour—both there 'up above' and in the hills whither he is returning home. All on earth below may fade and 'fall to the residuary worm'; but in heaven above he recognizes (as he says in *The Starlight Night*) the barn in which 'the shocks' are stored, the eternal dwelling of 'Christ and his mother and all his hallows'.

4
The Dearest Freshness

The world is charged with the grandeur of God.
　It will flame out, like shining from shook foil;
　It gathers to a greatness, like the ooze of oil
Crushed. Why do men then now not reck his rod?
Generations have trod, have trod, have trod;
　And all is seared with trade; bleared, smeared with toil;
　And wears man's smudge and shares man's smell: the soil
Is bare now, nor can foot feel, being shod.

And for all this, nature is never spent;
　There lives the dearest freshness deep down things;
And though the last lights off the black West went
　Oh, morning, at the brown brink eastward, springs—
Because the Holy Ghost over the bent
　World broods with warm breast and with ah! bright wings.

God's Grandeur

Deep in the heart no less of the poet himself than of the things he sees in the world of nature around him dwells 'the dearest freshness'. In spite of all that man does to the world, or in turn suffers from the world, this freshness remains and wells up like a spring, no less in him than in the world, from time to time. It is identified in the sonnet *The Sea and the Skylark* as 'that cheer and charm of earth's past prime', and in the contemporary sonnet *Spring* as

A strain of the earth's sweet being in the beginning
In Eden garden.

Looking in his characteristic manner from the temporal to the eternal beginning of things, and from created effects to their uncreated Cause,

34

Hopkins begins this first of his 'bright' series of sonnets with his axiomatic proposition: 'The world is charged with the grandeur of God.' In its general meaning this line is a variant of the words of Psalm 71: 'The whole earth shall be filled with his majesty.' But the poet significantly alters 'filled' (as a cup is filled with water) to 'charged' (as a battery is charged with electricity). In other words, he envisages the presence of God in the world in terms less of a substance (like water) than of a force (like electricity). He envisages God not just as present, but as actively present in his creatures, according to the third point made by Saint Ignatius Loyola in his 'Contemplation for Obtaining Divine Love': 'The third is to consider how God is at work and labours for my sake in all created things on the face of the earth . . .' On this point Hopkins has the following elaboration in his commentary on the *Spiritual Exercises*: 'All things therefore are charged with love, are charged with God and if we know how to touch them give off sparks and take fire, yield drops and flow, ring and tell of him.'

From this point of view, the world is seen as charged, not so much with the being or the infinity or the presence, as with the grandeur or the majesty of God. With the Psalmist, the poet sees the heavens as the throne of God and the earth as his footstool, while all things in the heavens and on earth reveal his glory and ring out his praises in one symphony of creation. As he declares in *The Wreck of the Deutschland*, he who is 'Lord of living and dead' is both present 'under the world's splendour and wonder' and

> throned behind
> Death with a sovereignty that heeds but hides, bodes but abides.

This divine grandeur, hidden though it may be from mortal sight, is yet manifested in a variety of ways. At times, it will 'flame out' in a sudden flash of splendour, 'like shining from shook foil'. This impressive flaming is also recognized by the poet in the way 'kingfishers catch fire, dragonflies draw flame', and still more in the way 'self flashes off frame and face' from what Blake calls 'the human form divine'. It is aptly expressed by him in connection with the word 'flash', whether used as a noun or a verb. The force of this word may be felt from two passages in *The Wreck of the Deutschland*: first, in the unusual phrase, 'brim, in a flash, full', where 'brim' and 'full' are component parts of the adjective 'brimful', each of them stressed and divided by the unstressed and swiftly recited 'in a flash'; and secondly, in the image of 'a released shower, let flash to the shire', for the characteristic action of God's mercy on man.

As for the simile, 'like shining from shook foil', Hopkins himself explains it in a letter to Bridges, dated 4 January 1883. After defining 'foil' as used here in its sense of leaf or tinsel, he says: 'Shaken gold foil gives off broad glares like sheet lightning and also, and this is true of nothing else, owing to its zigzag dents and creasings and network of small many-cornered facets, a sort of fork lightning too.' This comparison of the 'shining from shook foil' with lightning indicates the possibility of further associations in the poet's mind with the song of the thrush, as in *Spring*—'It strikes like lightnings to hear him sing'—and with the action of God, as described in *The Wreck of the Deutschland*: 'Thou art lightning and love, I found it.'

At other times, however, the grandeur of God manifests itself in a slow and gradual manner, 'gathering to a greatness' from small, almost imperceptible particles of presence. For this the poet elsewhere (in *The Wreck of the Deutschland*, stanza 10) uses the metaphor of spring stealing through the world of nature, appearing in a leaf here, a blossom there, in a cluster of shoots here, a bed of flowers there, till the whole face of the countryside is finally transformed in the month of May. But here he prefers an autumnal metaphor, from 'the ooze of oil' produced after the harvest of fruit. In this he is evidently inspired by Keats's description of the cider-press in his *Ode to Autumn*, with its 'last oozings, hours by hours'.

It is interesting to notice that in *The Wreck of the Deutschland* (stanza 10) the poet exemplifies these two apparently contrary, but really complementary, manifestations of God's grandeur in the lives of two saints. The first is shown in the experience of Saint Paul on the road to Damascus, as recorded in *Acts* ix: 'Whether at once, as once at a crash Paul'—where it is emphasized both by the sprung rhythm and by the echo of 'flash' in 'crash'. The second appears in the long-drawn-out process of Saint Augustine's conversion, as recorded in his *Confessions*: 'Or as Austin, a lingering-out swéet skíll'—where it is emphasized by the slow, anapaestic movement of the line, culminating in another use of sprung rhythm with a contrary effect. Of these two manifestations, the former shows forth the mastery of God, forging his will on rebellious man; and the latter, the mercy of God, melting the heart of man and so completing the work of mastery.

The poet now proceeds to develop the second of these manifestations by way of a coda to the metaphor of oil. For the oil is seen as coming out not only in the form of a gradual 'ooze', but also from fruit that has been 'crushed'. The reference of the metaphor is to fruit; but its metaphorical application is to men, of whom the poet now goes on to speak. Men, too, he implies, like fruit, have to be crushed so that God's grandeur may be manifested in them. The rebellious wills of men, he explains in *The*

Wreck of the Deutschland, God must wring with suffering and so bend them back to himself. Or as he elaborates in *Carrion Comfort*, God must bruise their bones with his 'wring-world right foot' and scan them with 'darksome devouring eyes'; he must fan their heap of mingled chaff and grain 'in turns of tempest', that their 'chaff might fly', their 'grain lie, sheer and clear'. Thus he will reveal his glory in them, as they come to recognize and to 'kiss the rod', that is, to accept his punishment as just and merciful, smiting and healing them in one and the same action.

It is in this context of thought that the following question has its point: 'Why do men then now not reck his rod?' Why is it, we find the poet similarly asking in *Ribblesdale*, that man is 'To his own selfbent so bound, so tied to his turn', as to 'none reck of world after'? Man is here seen as wild, wilful and wanton, in the excessive senses of these adjectives, where they connote nothing lovely, but only ugliness. Man is seen as the rebel who has come out not with the best, but with the worst word, not with 'Yes', but with 'No'; and who would, like Macbeth, have his be-all and end-all here on earth, and 'jump the life to come'. He is so hardened in sin, that he has become all but impervious to the rod of God's punishments.

Elsewhere this divine rod is vividly described, in *The Wreck of the Deutschland* (stanza 2) as a sweeping and hurling movement that 'trod / Hard down with a horror of height', and similarly in *Carrion Comfort*, as a 'heaven-handling' that 'flung me, fóot tród / Me', with an active, transitive force. But here it is described in terms of its effect on the successive generations of men, with an intransitive force: 'Generations have trod, have trod, have trod.' The dull repetition of the heavy monosyllabic verb makes an impressive thud on the ears. It emphasizes the monotony of a life lived without God and without hope in this world, the weary succession of day after day, 'Tomorrow and tomorrow and tomorrow', lived out 'To the last syllable of recorded time'. It also emphasizes the deeper truth that this monotony is itself a divine punishment coming down from above, like an iron weight crushing the rock-like heart of man and reducing him (literally) to contrition.

As things are now, the poet continues, 'all is seared with trade'. The iron has entered into the very soul of man, inured as he is to seeking his selfish profit in all things. All is now 'bleared, smeared with toil'. The senses of man have been dulled, numbed by constant labour, blinded to 'the things that are'. They no longer respond to earth's beauty, but are entering into 'night's blear-all black'. The things themselves have become smeared all over with dirt and grime from human toil, and have lost the freshness of their first being. On them are to be seen all over the ugly manmarks which 'treadmire toil there footfretted in it'. In a word, the foul smell not so much of human toil as of human selfishness has infected the whole material creation, over which man was originally constituted lord and master. The 'smudge' all things are now smeared with is no superficial mark: it amounts almost to deletion. The 'smell' all things are now impregnated with rises to high heaven, not as an odour of sweetness inviting God's blessing, but as a foul stench invoking his curse and retribution. This curse is at work in the very soil, depriving it of 'louchèd low grass' and beating it bare. Even if it were covered with grass, man would no longer appreciate its softness, his feet 'being shod' with shoes. Thus man is punished for his insensitivity to 'God's grandeur' by becoming correspondingly insensitive to the beauty of the natural world.

This gloomy description, arising out of the single word 'crushed', only serves to bring into stronger relief the supervening sestet. 'And for all this,' the poet goes on to emphasize, 'nature is never spent.' Let man do his worst, the resources of nature are never exhausted, her treasury never fully expended. There ever remains an unsuspected reserve of strength and resilience, in greater abundance than what seems to have been wasted. There is always 'the dearest freshness deep down things', an ever-springing source of beauty and love in the depths both of man and of nature. This is the meaning of the image Hopkins uses in another sonnet of this period, *The Starlight Night*:

> Down in dim woods the diamond delves! the elves'-eyes!
> The grey lawns cold where gold, where quickgold lies!

On the one hand, it is true, there is a continual decline in things, as Shakespeare insists in his Sonnet 73:

> That time of year thou mayst in me behold
> When yellow leaves, or none, or few, do hang
> Upon those boughs which shake against the cold . . .
>
> In me thou seest the twilight of such day
> As after sunset fadeth in the west,
> Which by and by black night doth take away . . .
>
> In me thou seest the glowing of such fire
> That on the ashes of his youth doth lie,
> As the death-bed whereon it must expire.

The lights that comfort human life go out one after another, and the last glimmerings of the departed sun gradually disappear. Similarly, the poet describes in *Spelt from Sibyl's Leaves* how the 'fond yellow horn-light' is 'wound to the west', and the 'wild hollow hoarlight' is 'hung to the height'; how the western horizon turns black, with 'beakleaved boughs' in the shape of dragons silhouetted against the 'bleak light' and seeming 'black, / Ever so black on it'—as an oracle of the life of man on earth. On the other hand, there is also a continual ascent in things, an upward force of renewal and resurrection. If the trees are un-leaving in Goldengrove, it is only to be clothed with fresh glory in the spring. If the sun sets in the west at the end of the day, it is only to reappear 'at the brown brink eastward' at the beginning of a new day. If the dying 'blue-bleak embers' expire in the fireplace at night, it is only to make room for another fire to be lit there, with fresh firecoals gleaming 'gold-vermilion' from the grate. The fading beauty of the 'dappled-with-damson west' is revived in the dayspring of a 'crimson-cresseted east'. And this, too, is an oracle of the life of man—if not on earth, at least in heaven.

By means of his metaphor of sunrise the poet moves to a triumphant climax, in which he explains his opening proposition in terms of this continual ascent in things. Why is it that 'nature is never spent'? Why is it that there 'lives the dearest freshness deep down things'? Why is it that, 'though the last lights off the black west went', yet 'morning, at the brown brink eastward springs'? Why? Because, the Holy Ghost, the Spirit of God himself, is continually and actively present in the world he has created, keeping it from returning to primeval nothingness. As in the beginning of creation he

> With mighty wings outspread
> Dove-like sat brooding o'er the vast Abyss

so ever since he continues to brood, day after day, year after year, generation after generation. He is not merely enthroned behind the world in passive splendour; but he actively broods over it, making it—as Milton aptly adds—pregnant. The world may be preoccupied with its own malice, 'to its own selfbent so bound'; but sooner or later God's goodness triumphs over man's malice, bending down to save man from himself—as a good shepherd bends down to gather up a torn lamb of his flock. He is the Spirit of Peace, traditionally represented under the symbol of a dove. He comes 'with work to do'—not just 'to coo', but 'to brood and sit'. He comes to brood and to bring forth his brood, like the 'Star-eyed strawberry-breasted / Throstle above her nested / Cluster of bugle blue eggs' in *The May Magnificat*. He comes to manifest the 'feathery delicacy' of 'lovely-felicitous providence', by whose means all men—'never ask if meaning it, wanting it, warned of it'—come under the feathers of their Father in heaven.

Thus in all creation, in its harsh no less than in its pleasing aspects, the poet feels the warmth of the divine breast and glimpses the brightness of the divine wings. This is far more than a notional recognition on his part, based on an abstract faith in the presence and providence of God. Rather, it seems to rise, in the climax of this poem, to the level of a mystical experience, as he first feels the warmth of the breast, and then sees—with an 'ah!' of ecstatic wonder—the brightness of the wings, at least in a momentary glimpse which is all that this world can afford.

5
Dappled Things

Glory be to God for dappled things—
　　For skies of couple-colour as a brinded cow;
　　　　For rose-moles all in stipple upon trout that swim;
Fresh-firecoal chestnut-falls; finches' wings;
　　Landscape plotted and pieced—fold, fallow, and plough;
　　　　And áll trádes, their gear and tackle and trim.

All things counter, original, spare, strange;
　　Whatever is fickle, freckled (who knows how?)
　　　　With swift, slow; sweet, sour; adazzle, dim;
He fathers-forth whose beauty is past change:
　　　　　　Praise him.

Pied Beauty

The material object of Hopkins's poetic vision, in the full meaning of the phrase, is beauty in all its many-sided variety. In his discussion of the purpose of mortal beauty he argues that, however it may fade in the course of time, it still serves to keep warm 'men's wits to the things that are'—to maintain them in life-giving contact with being and with goodness. This beauty he finds, as a poet in the Romantic tradition, rather in nature than in art, and rather in the wild and wanton than in the tame or domestic aspects of nature. This is why he particularly admires the 'barbarous' beauty of the stooks in the harvested fields of autumn, the 'brute' beauty of the windhover caught in a glimpse one morning, the 'wild' beauty of the 'darksome burn' at Inversnaid. Conversely, he has little use for classical simplicity or geometrical balance. Rather, he delights in the variety and profusion of riches in the natural world, which observes a form of balance but with stresses of a far more complex kind than are to be found in the geometry of Euclid. He recognizes that all colours may be resolved into the simplicity of white light; but he prefers to enjoy them for the time being in all their variety. It is as if he feels himself unable to appreciate the rich simplicity of the Creator, until he has fully delighted in the complexity of his creatures.

Created beauty is thus for Hopkins essentially 'pied beauty'—beauty that is intricately interwoven with white and black, light and darkness, summer and winter, day and night, heaven and earth. Upon this fundamental contrast supervene the varied colours of the rainbow, even as the rising of the sun over the earth imparts to all things a dappled or mottled appearance and diversifies them in almost unlimited individuality. 'Earth's dapple' is particularly apparent in the morning, when the 'dapple-dawn-drawn Falcon' rides forth on the 'steady air', and in the spring-time, 'When drop-of-blood-and-foam-dapple / Bloom lights the orchard-apple'—in contrast to the preceding night, and winter-time. It is again apparent in the evening, when the sun sets in 'the dappled-with-damson west', and in the autumn, when there is sadness over 'Goldengrove unleaving'—in view of the approach of night, and of winter. At the same time, beneath the dapple and thingness of 'dappled things' the poet adores the simplicity of God, who is 'all in all'; 'under the world's splendour and wonder' he recognizes the presence of God, whose 'mystery must be instressed, stressed'. So it is that in all and above all he gives 'glory to God for dappled things'.

This simple opening of his sonnet echoes the motto or axiom given by Saint Ignatius Loyola to the members of the Society of Jesus: *Ad Majorem Dei Gloriam*—'To the greater glory of God'. This motto, in its abbreviated form of *A.M.D.G.*, boys at Jesuit schools in Hopkins's time were required to write at the beginning of every written exercise for their masters. Similarly, at the end of every exercise they were required to write another motto, *Laus Deo Semper*—'Praise be to God always'—in its abbreviated form of *L.D.S.* Hopkins, too, in this sonnet moves from the motto, 'Glory be to God', to the concluding motto, 'Praise him'— almost as if regarding his poem as a school exercise. In this case, the exercise may be seen as one of logic, passing from the general to the particular in order of argumentation, and then again from the particular to the general in the conclusion. Only by framing the whole exercise between the two mottoes, the whole becomes a prayer of praise and a meditation on the glory of God in his creatures.

In the course of his descent from the general to the particular, and from the glory of God to 'dappled things', the poet first rests his eyes on 'skies of couple-colour'—finding in them the dapple of blue and white, which are for him Mary's colours. Similarly, in the climax of *The Wreck of the Deutschland* he admires 'the jay-blue heavens appearing / Of pied and peeled May', and specifies the dappled contrast of 'Blue-beating and hoary-glow height' in them. This blue, he notes in his metaphysical poem on *The Blessed Virgin Compared to the Air we Breathe*, is the native colour of the 'azurèd' air and serves to slake the fierce fire of the sun, which else 'would shake, / A blear and blinding ball / With blackness bound'. So, too, Mary's motherly love, encompassing us like the air, serves to avert from us sinners the fire of God's anger. The white, with which the blue is pleasantly variegated, may take the hazy form of a 'hoary glow', or the more precise form of 'silk-sack clouds'. Oddly enough, however, the 'couple-colour' of the skies is here compared to 'a brinded cow', with its blending of brown and white. At first sight, there would seem to be no special connection between skies and cows—apart from the nursery rhyme. But one may imagine the poet 'in a fine frenzy' rolling his eye from heaven to earth, from the clouds in the sky to the cows in the meadow, from the dapple of blue and white to the similar dapple of brown and white. There is also an assonantal connection of words: 'dappled' is echoed in 'couple-colour', and 'things' in 'brinded', while 'cow' continues the alliteration of 'skies of couple-colour' on a softer, palatal level after the hard, guttural opening of 'Glory be to God'.

Pursuing the same imaginative line of thought, one may follow the poet's eye from the meadow to a stream by the meadow, and from the cow grazing in the meadow to trout swimming in the stream. As with the cow, so with the trout, what he particularly notices is the dappled appearance of their skin, marked as it is with 'rose-moles all in stipple'— that is, with spotted configurations. Possibly it was for such trout that he went fishing in the river Elwy; but here he is interested not in catching, but in contemplating them—or only in catching them as he 'caught' the wind-hover—while swimming in their watery element. Further, beside the meadow and beneath the trees his eyes comes to rest on chestnuts— probably, the nuts or 'conkers' of horse-chestnuts—that have fallen to the ground and burst open. Within the 'chestnut-falls' (a word he has formed on analogy with 'windfalls' from fruit-trees) he finds gleaming brown nuts, which he aptly compares to fresh coals of fire. The whole discovery he compresses into the alliterative compound, 'Fresh-firecoal chestnut-falls'. Its fuller implications may be unfolded by comparison with *The Windhover*, where the poet describes how 'blue-bleak embers' (like the chestnuts from the tree) 'Fall, gall themselves, and gash gold-vermilion'; and with *The Wreck of the Deutschland*, where the poet speaks of God's 'fall-gold mercies' and his 'all-fire glances'. Here the dapple is between the tan of the husk and the 'fresh-firecoal' of the kernel; while in the kernel itself there is a further contrast between gold and vermilion, implicit here but explicit in the parallel passage of *The Windhover*.

Still following the poet's eye in imagination, we pass from the ground below to the tree above—as in the sonnet on *Spring*—and there we notice birds on the branches. In *Spring* and *The May Magnificat* he refers explicitly to the thrush, and in two other sonnets he devotes his special attention to the skylark—mainly for their song. But here he dwells rather on the dappled appearance of 'finches' wings'—whether they be chaffinches, or bullfinches, or goldfinches. Another reason for the selection of 'finches' here may have been the alliteration with 'fresh-firecoal chestnut-falls'. Finally, from this precise focus on 'finches' wings' he extends his survey to the whole surrounding countryside, as it would have appeared to him from his point of vantage at St Beuno's College. From there he could easily move his eyes to the 'Landscape plotted and pieced', spread out before him like a patchwork quilt or eiderdown. Some of the fields there would be used as pasture for sheep to graze in—'fold'. Others would be left unused to recuperate their energies for another sowing—'fallow'. Yet others would have been turned up for the growing of crops, and would be in different stages of growth—'plough'. Together they would all form the 'dappled' panoramic inscape of the Vale of Clwyd.

In viewing such a landscape, the poet's attention would be drawn not only to the world of nature, but also to the works of man, as he acts upon that world 'in the sweat of his brow'. Among these works the agricultural would be most in evidence, in the 'landscape plotted and pieced', as being most deeply rooted in human nature 'from life's dawn'. But they in turn are varied with the industrial works, of which there would also be indications in the towns scattered through the valley—Denbigh, St Asaph, and Rhyl. This thought is what prompts the further mention of 'all trades', not now in the derogatory sense implied in *God's Grandeur*, but in the orderly association evoked by 'their gear and tackle and trim'. Beneath these generalities the poet is evidently thinking of his preferred pastime of fishing, both on the individual scale of an angler, who needs 'tackle', and on the wider scale of fishing-boats and trawlers, whose 'gear' has to be kept in good 'trim.'

After a short octet of only six lines there follows a proportionately shortened sestet of four and a half lines, to make up what Hopkins has christened a 'curtal sonnet'. To the substantive examples he has listed in the octet he now adds a series of descriptive adjectives. He descants, as it were, on the meaning of 'dappled things', as all things that are 'counter, original, spare, strange'—in other words, all things that stand in contrast with other things, that are unique in themselves, that are rarely to be found in the world, that arouse surprise when they are found or looked at afresh. In such terms he expresses his characteristic fascination by whatever is odd or eccentric, partly because of a similar quality in himself. Incidentally, it was this quality in him that is recalled in an anecdote of his sojourn at Stonyhurst, where he was observed by one of the lay brothers standing on a path and looking fixedly at something on the ground before him. Yet it is not merely the oddity of eccentricity or things that fascinates him, but the contrast or 'piedness' with what is normal and ordinary in them.

He goes on to express his delight in whatever is 'fickle', like the English weather, or 'freckled', like the faces of some children. With them perhaps in mind he adds the charming question, 'who knows how?' (in parenthesis)—as it were echoing the question in the children's rhyme: 'Why has a cow got four legs?' It is, of course, a rhetorical question, like the series of questions asked by God in the *Book of Job*, of which the answer is known to God alone. It is noticeable, moreover, that through all these adjectives the poet is moving from 'all things' to men, as being 'world's loveliest—men's selves'. The final adjective, 'freckled', is not—as may appear at first sight, because of the following parenthesis—used absolutely, in the sense of covered with freckles, but relatively, in connection with the pairs of contrasting adjectives that occupy the next line. In them the poet is applying his love of 'piedness' to adjectives, no less than to the nouns they qualify. Also in them he is following an order of images that corresponds to that in Part the First of *The Wreck of the Deutschland*. Thus in 'swift, slow', there may well be a reference to the river of time, which the stress and stroke of God rides masterfully, and so to the contrary, or complementary, ways of God's dealings with men: swift, 'as once at a crash Paul', and slow, 'as Austin, a lingering-out swéet skíll'. There is also a sound-association between 'slow' and the 'lush-kept plush-capped sloe' which bursts in the mouth and flushes 'the man, the being with it, sour or sweet'. Thus it serves to suggest the next pair of 'sweet, sour', which contains the implication of 'the best or worst word'— 'yes' or 'no'. Thirdly, in 'adazzle, dim', there is a clear echo of the 'dark descending' of God, which is later described (in stanza 34) in negative terms as 'Not a dooms-day dazzle in his coming nor dark as he came'.

Thus, like the 'dappled things' in the natural world, these contrasting pairs of adjectives are not merely chosen at random, but follow an underlying pattern according to the order of God's providence. First, there comes the stress and stroke of God's creative action in the world, swift as a mountain torrent, as in the 'dense and the driven Passion', and then slow as a wide river flowing past green meadows, 'in high flood yet'. This is followed by man's response to God's action, whether sweet in acceptance, or sour in rejection. Finally, God descends to earth in judgment, to reward or to punish, either gently as 'a released shower, let

45

flash to the shire', or terribly as 'a dooms-day dazzle in his coming' and 'a lightning of fire hard-hurled'—though even in the latter case the poet prays that he may be most merciful then.

The conclusion of the sonnet is, therefore, that all this variety of mortal beauty must proceed from him whom Saint Paul recognizes as the source of all fatherhood in heaven and on earth—the immortal source of all that is mortal. Earthly beauty may be fickle; but in its fickleness there is something that charms us by virtue of him 'whose beauty is past change'. Earthly beauty may be dappled; but in its dappledness there is something that reminds us of him who is perfectly simple and without differentiation. All good attributes of creatures, however diverse among themselves, are somehow—as Hopkins learnt from Duns Scotus—fully present and united in the rich simplicity of the divine being. Similarly, all good things and perfect gifts—as Hopkins learnt, not only from Saint James, but also from Saint Ignatius Loyola in his 'Contemplation for Obtaining Divine Love'—'descend from above, as my poor power from the supreme and infinite power above, and similarly, justice, goodness, pity, mercy, etc. just as from the sun descend rays, from the fountain waters, etc.'

All these considerations terminate somewhat abruptly in the coda of practical exhortation: 'Praise him.' Here one may find an echo of the opening line of Newman's famous hymn (with a not impossible pun on 'hymn'): 'Praise to the holiest in the height'. But the primary reference of these two words is (as we have already seen) to Saint Ignatius's motto, *Laus Deo Semper.* In this brief exhortation, everything in the poem, as in the world of nature, is drawn to a point, in which all creatures contribute, as well by their varied sounds as by their show of 'pied beauty', to the grand symphony of praise in honour of their Creator.

6

Dapple-Dawn-Drawn Falcon

To Christ our Lord

I caught this morning morning's minion, king-
    dom of daylight's dauphin, dapple-dawn-drawn Falcon, in his
      riding
    Of the rolling level underneath him steady air, and striding
High there, how he rung upon the rein of a wimpling wing
In his ecstasy! then off, off forth on swing,
    As a skate's heel sweeps smooth on a bow-bend: the hurl and
      gliding
    Rebuffed the big wind. My heart in hiding
Stirred for a bird,—the achieve of, the mastery of the thing!

Brute beauty and valour and act, oh, air, pride, plume, here
    Buckle! AND the fire that breaks from thee then, a billion
Times told lovelier, more dangerous, O my chevalier!

    No wonder of it: shéer plód makes plough down sillion
Shine, and blue-bleak embers, ah my dear,
    Fall, gall themselves, and gash gold-vermilion.

The Windhover

The poetic theory of Hopkins, with its characteristic emphasis on the 'inscape' (or inner form) of nature and the 'instress' (or inner vitality) of things, has its supreme illustration in *The Windhover*, the poem which he regarded (at least, as of 22 June 1879) as 'the best thing I ever wrote'. In other sonnets, composed during his 'bright' period at St Beuno's College, he dwells on the various inscapes he delights to find in nature: on the spectacle of a starlight night, on the varied beauty of spring, on the general consideration of pied beauty, and on his personal response of 'hurrahing' in harvest time. He reflects, too, on the animal life around him—particularly in *The Sea and the Skylark*, and *The Caged Skylark*—and draws appropriate moral and religious conclusions. Above all, within and above all natural inscapes, he reflects on human beings, whose passing by he finds symbolized in a *Lantern out of Doors*. In none of these sonnets, however, does he succeed in capturing the instress of a particular event in nature so skilfully, or in applying it to his own peculiar position so aptly, as in *The Windhover*.

Here the poet concentrates more attentively than ever before on a single moment of high instress in the flight of a kestrel, whom he calls in the title of his poem 'The Windhover' (with the definite article, of a particular bird), and in the poem itself 'Falcon' (with a capital F, as for a person). The name in the title would have been familiar to him during his sojourn at St Beuno's, from an inscription on a glass case of stuffed birds which was subsequently removed to Stonyhurst College in 1887. It reads: 'The Kestrel or Windhover: The commonest and most conspicuous of British falcons remarkable for its habit of remaining suspended in the air without changing position while it scans the ground for its prey.' Thus the title of the poem, as well as the further name of Falcon, may well have been derived from this glass case. But the contents of the poem can only have come from the experience of 'the thing' in nature, combined with the interpretation provided by the poet's meditation on the Kingdom of Christ in the *Spiritual Exercises* of Saint Ignatius Loyola. From this meditation he evidently derived the terms of medieval chivalry scattered in his poem, the whole movement of thought from the composition of place in the octet to the colloquy in the sestet, and above all, the ultimate dedication of the sonnet (in its final version) 'To Christ our Lord'. From his experience, however, he derived the description to which he devotes the whole octet with an unusual (even for Hopkins) intensity of purpose.

Already in his opening phrase 'I caught', a wealth of meaning is implicit. Ostensibly it means 'I caught sight of', or rather, 'I caught a glimpse of'—referring to an event or situation that is essentially momentary and fleeting in time. At a deeper level, it also means the fact that the poet has recaptured the 'fine careless rapture' of the bird within the compass of his poem by means of a carefully selected consort of words and rhythms. There is already something arresting in the sound of the verb 'caught', with its monosyllabic abruptness, that catches the attention of the reader as well and directs it insistently towards the object of the verb with all its local and temporal circumstances.

The temporal circumstance of the sonnet is 'this morning', with its implication shortly to be developed of the tingling freshness of early

Bluebells at St Beuno's
Below Fretty chervil
Previous page Kestrel (in the Stonyhurst collection)

Abeles at St Beuno's
Below The valley of the Ribble, Yorkshire
Overleaf Sunset at St Beuno's

Opposite Binsey poplars
Below Golden maple in the autumn and in the winter (at West Baden, USA)

Goldengrove, Clwyd
Below The spires of Oxford

dawn. This serves to introduce the object of the verb, not immediately, but at the end of a procession of titles, as in some royal proclamation of medieval pageantry. First comes the title of 'morning's minion', or darling—with overtones of a royal favourite, as was Piers Gaveston to Edward II of England. There follows 'kingdom of daylight's dauphin', or crown prince and heir to the throne of France, the source and wellspring of medieval chivalry. Finally, the bird is himself introduced, not with the generic and prosaic name of kestrel, but with the high-sounding name of Falcon, spelt with a capital F to suggest a person. He is also accompanied by an appropriate attribute of light—not just the general 'morning' with 'minion', nor the heraldic 'kingdom of daylight' with 'dauphin', but more precisely and naturally, 'dapple-dawn-drawn'. What has impelled him forth at this early hour is the dappled dawn, with all its varied inscape, elsewhere characterized by Hopkins as the 'crimson-cresseted east' (in *The Wreck of the Deutschland* stanza 35) and as 'the brown brink eastward' whence the dayspring appears (in *God's Grandeur*).

Now with the imagery of medieval chivalry uppermost in his mind, from the words 'minion' and 'dauphin' and 'Falcon', the poet goes on to envisage the bird in terms of a rider on his horse. In doing so, he instinctively recurs to the speech of another Dauphin, in Shakespeare's *Henry V* (iii.7), where the latter gives a glowing description (in prose) of his horse:

> He bounds from the earth, as if his entrails were hairs; le cheval volant, the Pegasus, chez les narines de feu! When I bestride him, I soar, I am a hawk: he trots the air; the earth sings when he touches it. . . . It is a beast for Perseus: he is pure air and fire; and the dull elements of earth and water never appear in him, but only in patient stillness while his rider mounts him.

Only, whereas the Dauphin speaks of his horse in terms of a hawk, Hopkins reverses the metaphor and speaks of his Falcon, 'towering in her pride of place' (to use Shakespeare's other words in *Macbeth* ii.4), in terms of a horseman 'in his riding'. In his metaphor, the horse is 'the rolling level underneath him steady air', that is, the air which the bird seems to ride without effort and which remains, for all its rolling, level and steady under his firm control of the reins. As for the Falcon, he bestrides his horse, seated majestically in the saddle 'High there'—not just statically as in an equestrian portrait, but dynamically as 'he rung upon the rein of a wimpling wing'. There is a combination of physical power and intellectual skill in his momentary motionlessness, as he hovers in the wind— like an expert trainer pulling on the rein of a fierce, untamed animal in a ring and forcing it to keep within the limits of the rein he holds. The rein

49

itself is identified as the 'wimpling wing', extended in flight and rippling (like a nun's wimple) in the wind, since it is by its mighty wings outspread that the Falcon controls the force of the wind and uses it for its flight. There is thus an intense, if unseen, struggle, a pitting of strength between mighty opposites, the bird on the one hand and the wind on the other, such as the poet elsewhere describes in terms of the Biblical wrestling between Jacob and the Angel: 'And the midriff astrain with leaning of, laced with fire of stress' (*The Wreck of the Deutschland* stanza 2; cf. also *Carrion Comfort*). In this struggle the bird maintains his mastery over the wind, and from it he derives a feeling of ecstasy, which is in turn conveyed to the watching poet, and by him to his readers.

What follows in the second quatrain is a swift movement consequent on the static tension of the hovering: as the bird 'hovers off', gliding on the wings of the wind, but still subduing it to his own purpose. This movement is described as a 'swing'—like 'the swing of the sea', in the early poem *Heaven–Haven*. Its quality is conveyed above all by the sprung rhythm of the line. From the 'ecstasy' with which it begins, there follows a breathless pause—'then off', with three successive stresses on as many syllables, as it were repeated exertions of force: 'off, off forth'— bearing issue in the free 'swing' of the bird down the wind. It reminds the poet of the graceful movement of an experienced skater, performing a figure of eight on the ice, as he swings round at the 'bow-bend'. In it he finds a paradoxical combination of dynamic effort in 'the hurl' and effortless impetus in 'gliding'. In either case, the bird (like the skater) is perfect master of the situation, rebuffing the force of 'the big wind' with his superior skill.

Now at last the poet has leisure to reflect on his own 'heart in hiding'. In this phrase he may be thinking of himself watching the bird from a place of hiding on the ground below; or of his heart hiding (as he puts it in *The Wreck of the Deutschland* stanza 18) in its 'bower of bone' and 'turned for an exquisite smart'; or else of his situation 'on a pastoral forehead of Wales', leading a life hidden from men of the world where 'honour is flashed off exploit'. Anyhow, in his heart he feels a deep stirring of admiration at the achievement and the mastery of the bird in his superb control of the wind. In his admiration there is also perhaps an element of envy, contrasting the 'act' of the bird with his own apparent inactivity in his life of study and prayer at St Beuno's, which is (as he notes in his *Devotional Writings*) 'obscure, constrained, and unsuccessful'. Yet the main emphasis of his reflection is not introverted, but looking out from himself to the 'achieve' and the 'mastery' of what he can only call 'the thing'. To some this may seem a weak word, as being too general; but to Hopkins it is strong precisely in its generality or universality, emphasizing the concrete actuality or (what he calls in *Duns Scotus's Oxford*) 'realty' of the event.

This climax of the octet, with its resounding emphasis on 'the thing', is now contrasted with the subjective reflection that ensues in the sestet. First, the poet sums up the qualities of the bird which he so admires: its brute beauty, its masculine courage, its intense actuality—in the fullest Aristotelian sense of *energeia*. In its flight he finds not only the beauty of natural inscape, where 'all's to one thing wrought', but also the force of individual instress, which wells up from the very source of created existence. Well may the bird give itself airs, take pride in its mastery, and plume itself on its achievement, allowing for its wild and wanton condition. But as for himself he now recognizes a far wider possibility of mastery and achievement open to him as man, even as his human nature is far nobler than the animal nature of the bird. There is, after all, no need of envy: his is a far higher vocation. Paradoxically, it is to be achieved not by mastery, but by service: not by the exertion of physical strength, or even of intellectual skill, in the eyes of an admiring multitude, but by the renunciation of merely natural powers in obedience to a higher, supernatural ideal, the service of 'Christ our Lord'.

This is the general context of thought in which we have to determine the precise significance of the much disputed words, 'here / Buckle! AND'. Each of these words has been subjected to a bewildering diversity of interpretation; and no doubt the poet himself has deliberately shrouded the precise significance of his words in an ambiguity that is rich and pregnant. Thus 'here' may refer to the bird 'in his ecstasy', or to the poet's 'heart in hiding', or to the situation as a whole. 'Buckle' may mean 'clasp together', as in buckling on a belt, or 'come to grips', as in buckling to a task or a battle, or else 'crumple up in submission', as in buckling up or buckling under a superior. 'AND' may be merely copulative after an indicative verb, or consequential after an imperative verb. In addition, one has also to account for the interjection 'oh', the exclamation-mark after 'Buckle', and the capitalization of 'AND'— without metrical stress to justify it. Finally, the ensuing 'thee' with the vocative 'O my chevalier' may refer either to Christ, to whom the poem is dedicated, or to the poet himself, as addressing his own heart, or conceivably to the bird seen as a symbol of Christ. Out of all these possibilities a consistent line of interpretation has to be drawn in view of the total context of the poem and of Hopkins's poetic practice in other poems, in view also of the poem's dependence on the meditation of the Kingdom of Christ and on the *Spiritual Exercises* as a whole.

To begin with, the poet is turning his attention in the sestet from 'the thing' in the world of nature to his own 'heart in hiding', and from the realm of nature to that of grace. He is thinking primarily of himself, and exhorting himself to put off his natural envy at the 'Brute beauty and valour and act' he so admires in the bird, and to 'Buckle' his natural pride under the supernatural ideal of serving Christ the King. It is precisely to this ideal that Saint Ignatius leads him in the third point of his meditation on the Kingdom, where the exercitant, after following the parable of the King and his campaign, is encouraged to make a personal application of it to himself as a knight, or 'chevalier', of Christ.

> Those who wish to show more affection to Christ the King and to be outstanding in all service of their eternal King and universal Lord, will not only offer themselves entirely to a life of labour, but by acting against their own sensuality, their carnal and worldly love, will make offerings of greater value and importance.

In keeping with this interpretation, the 'oh' is an expression of intense desire, as in *Henry Purcell*: 'Let him oh! with his air of angels then lift me, lay me!' Likewise the exclamation-mark after 'Buckle!' points rather to an imperative (of command) or an optative (of desire), than to an indicative (of statement). As for the capitalization of 'AND', it serves to emphasize the apodosis (sequel) of the condition implied in the imperative or optative: *if* the command is obeyed, or *if* the desire is fulfilled, *then* . . . Consequently, 'Buckle' primarily means 'buckle under' in humble submission to Christ the King; with the possible secondary meanings of 'buckle on', or come together under Christ, and of 'buckle to', or join battle with Christ against his enemies. In further consequence, 'thee' must refer to the poet's 'heart in hiding' at St Beuno's, where he is training for the hurtle of 'fiercest fray' as a 'chevalier' in the service of Christ.

Once this condition is fulfilled, not in the bird, nor in Christ, but in the poet united to Christ in humble service, *then* the fire of divine love that will break from him will be immeasurably lovelier and more effective— more 'dangerous' against his spiritual enemies, the devil, the world and the flesh—than the 'brute beauty' he has witnessed in the windhover. To worldly ears this may seem merely pious exaggeration; but for the poet it is a simple statement of fact—'No wonder of it'. So he goes on to substantiate his statement with two examples from the world of nature.

The first of these examples, suggested by the words of Christ about putting one's hand to the plough, and borrowed in its details from Virgil's *Georgics I*, points to the paradox of a ploughshare that comes out shining from the muddy earth of the furrow it has just been ploughing. This meaning is skilfully brought out by the very choice and order of words, as the heaviness of 'pl' in 'plod' and 'plough' is succeeded by the softness of 's' in 'sillion' (from the French *sillon*) and 'shine'. The final word receives additional emphasis from its position at the beginning of the following line. The general sense implied in this example is that the poet has set his hand to the plough in Christ's service, and has felt the temptation (by envying the bird) to look back in regret; but he now reminds himself that in the arduous labour of ploughing there is hidden the light of grace, and that what he sows in tears he will reap in joy.

The second example, of the dying embers of a fire, may have been suggested by Shakespeare's Sonnet 73:

> In me thou see'st the glowing of such fire
> That on the ashes of his youth doth lie.

The embers are now 'blue' with cold and 'bleak' in their aspect; and this, again, is how the poet is tempted to feel about his hidden life in religion. He therefore speaks to himself, or perhaps Christ speaks to him in his heart, echoing the words of George Herbert in his well-known poem *Love*: 'I the unkinde, ungratefull? Ah my deare, I cannot look on thee.' These words are put by Hopkins in the mouth of Love, who also takes his hand and shows him how the embers as they fall (by analogy with human suffering), even in the act of galling themselves, break open and reveal the hidden glory or 'gold-vermilion' of fire (or Divine Love). This is the movement of thought we find in the imagery of *The Wreck of the Deutschland* stanza 23, where it is by their drowning and death that the sisters come to 'bathe in his fall-gold mercies' and 'breathe in his all-fire glances'. (Here 'fall-gold' has the combined implication of the golden colours of autumn and of the golden fire within a falling ember.)

Everything in the sestet—and indeed in the poem as a whole—thus leads up to the final revelation of 'gold-vermilion', as it were the precious discovery (already hinted at in *The Starlight Night*) of 'diamond delves' and 'elves'-eyes' in 'The grey lawns cold where gold, where quickgold lies'. This is the fundamental lesson of the particular meditation of the Kingdom, and of the spiritual teaching of Saint Ignatius in general—the lesson he draws both from the hidden life of Jesus at Nazareth and from all the labours and sufferings of Christ in his public life and passion, on which Hopkins himself comments in a sermon for 23 November, 1879: 'Poor was his station, laborious his life, bitter his ending: through poverty, through labour, through crucifixion his majesty of nature more shines.' From this point of view, the sestet is to be seen as a colloquy addressed by the poet, not to Christ, but to his own heart, arising out of the experience described in the octet. But then, following the advice of Saint Ignatius, he takes the colloquy in its completed form and dedicates it 'To Christ our Lord' in token of perfect submission to his loving will.

7
Banks and Brakes

May is Mary's month, and I
Muse at that and wonder why:
   Her feasts follow reason,
   Dated due to season—

Candlemas, Lady Day;
But the Lady Month, May,
   Why fasten that upon her,
   With a feasting in her honour?

Is it only its being brighter
Than the most are must delight her?
   Is it opportunest
   And flowers finds soonest?

Ask of her, the mighty mother:
Her reply puts this other
   Question: What is Spring?—
   Growth in everything—

Flesh and fleece, fur and feather,
Grass and greenworld all together;
   Star-eyed strawberry-breasted
   Throstle above her nested

Cluster of bugle blue eggs thin
Forms and warms the life within;
   And bird and blossom swell
   In sod or sheath or shell.

All things rising, all things sizing
Mary sees, sympathising
 With that world of good,
 Nature's motherhood.

Their magnifying of each its kind
With delight calls to mind
 How she did in her stored
 Magnify the Lord.

Well but there was more than this:
Spring's universal bliss
 Much, had much to say
 To offering Mary May.

When drop-of-blood-and-foam-dapple
Bloom lights the orchard-apple
 And thicket and thorp are merry
 With silver-surfèd cherry,

And azuring-over greybell makes
Wood banks and brakes wash wet like lakes
 And magic cuckoocall
 Caps, clears, and clinches all—

This ecstasy all through mothering earth
Tells Mary her mirth till Christ's birth
 To remember and exultation
 In God who was her salvation.

The May Magnificat

The inspiration breathing through the 'bright sonnets' is clearly that of spring and summer—from the time there appears 'a May-mess, like on orchard boughs' to the time of harvest when, 'barbarous in beauty, the stooks rise'. But it is on the earlier time that Hopkins lays the greater emphasis. For him 'Nothing is so beautiful as Spring'. Then it is that he gazes on the ground at his feet, and sees with wonder how 'weeds, in wheels, shoot long and lovely and lush'. Then it is that he looks in the hedgerow and observes how 'Thrush's eggs look little low heavens'. Then it is that he listens to the song of the thrush, which

Through the echoing timber does so rinse and wring
The ear, it strikes like lightnings to hear him sing.

Then it is that through the 'leaves and blooms' of the 'glassy peartree' he sees and feels 'the descending blue' of the sky, as it were 'all in a rush / With richness'; while from the earth below he senses the thrust that tosses 'the racing lambs' as they 'have fair their fling'.

This is the time of the year when 'the dearest freshness deep down things' rises again to the surface of nature; and the earth is young once more, thanks to

A strain of the earth's sweet being in the beginning
In Eden garden.

This is the time of 'the heart's cheering', when the 'down-dugged ground-hugged grey' of winter finally 'Hovers off'; and in its place there appear 'the jay-blue heavens . . . Of pied and peeled May'. This is also the time of the year that is traditionally consecrated to Mary, 'the mighty mother'; and it is on the inner meaning of this consecration that the poet dwells in one of his brightest poems, though not a sonnet, *The May Magnificat*.

As a member of the Society of Jesus, Hopkins cherished a special devotion to the Mother of Jesus; and of her he makes frequent mention in his poems. It was partly through this devotion that he felt drawn to the theology of Duns Scotus, in whom he recognized

Of realty the rarest-veinèd unraveller; a not
Rivalled insight, be rival Italy or Greece;
Who fired France for Mary without spot.

This last line refers to Scotus's celebrated defence of the thesis of Mary's Immaculate Conception, which was then much debated in medieval universities, and which was later warmly supported by the Jesuit theologians from the sixteenth century onwards. It was, moreover, the feast of the Immaculate Conception, which had but recently been instituted for the universal Church on 8 December, that largely inspired Hopkins in his composition of *The Wreck of the Deutschland*. For this 'was the feast followed the night' of the shipwreck, the 'Feast of the one woman without stain' of original sin; and it was by following Mary's example that the nun who called on Christ in the storm 'heard and kept thee and uttered thee outright'. Thus there is a direct line of influence from Mary in her response to the Angel, through the nun in her call to Christ, to the poet in his composition of the poem.

With all this in his mind Hopkins, now no longer at St Beuno's but back at Stonyhurst in the spring of 1878, ponders on the fact that 'May is Mary's month' and wonders why it is so—'Why fasten that upon her, / With a feasting in her honour?' Other feasts of hers, he reflects, occur on particular days, celebrating various events of her life in connection with the mysteries of the incarnate Son of God. But here is a whole month set aside in her honour, not indeed in the official liturgy of the Church, but in the popular devotion of Christians. So the poet searches in his mind for an answer, considering various possibilities in much the same spirit as when he considered the possible meanings of the nun's call to Christ in the storm. Thus it is that he observes the Jesuit tradition of offering 'May verses' to Mary during this month.

This time, however, he rejects none of the possibilities he considers, but lets them stand. Only the first two are insufficient, as being too extrinsic and general. It is not merely that May is 'brighter / Than the most are', or that it is the 'opportunest' time of the year for finding flowers to deck her altars. It is rather that in the very nature of spring, at its height in May, there is an underlying analogy with Mary as Mother of God. She is ' the mighty mother', replacing in the Christian dispensation the Great Mother of the ancient religions, Cybele, Demeter and Isis. So to the question, 'What is Spring?' the poet gives the simple answer, 'Growth in everything'—as it were, under the influence of her who is Mother of God.

In this wider context Hopkins now returns to his description of the hedgerows in May-time as he had given it in his sonnet on *Spring*. He begins by enumerating the various kinds of growth: of 'flesh', in boys and girls with 'Innocent mind and Mayday'; of 'fleece', in lambs as they 'have fair their fling'; of 'fur', in other animals; of 'feather', in the thrush singing from 'the glassy peartree'; of 'grass', in the 'louched low grass' of *Ribblesdale*; and of 'greenworld', in the woodland and forest all together. Among all these creatures, with 'all this juice and all this joy', he once again selects his favourite thrush for special mention—the 'throstle', or song-thrush, whose eyes he compares to stars, and whose breast to strawberries. He represents her not as singing, like her mate in *Spring*, but as sitting on her 'Cluster of bugle blue eggs thin' in her nest. In his earlier poem he had compared her eggs to 'little low heavens'; but here he associates their colour, 'bugle blue', with the starry flowers of the bugle on the ground below. Within them, he reflects, the life is being formed and warmed by the mother bird. Not only the chicks in their shells, but the shoots in their earthy sods and the blossoms in their green sheaths are swelling to the fullness of size—when they finally come 'out with it' and 'brim, in a flash, full'.

All these things the poet sees in their 'rising' and their 'sizing', and Mary, too, he says, sees them with her motherly sympathy and creative recognition that 'they are very good'. In them he, and Mary too, finds the mysterious working of 'nature's motherhood', as nature bears them all in her womb and finally brings them to birth in the month of May 'with delight'. Looking on them thus with her eyes and her mind, he recognizes the underlying analogy between this motherhood of nature repeated from year to year and the motherhood of Mary which happened once and for all. What happened in the order of grace at Nazareth and Bethlehem, in what Eliot calls an 'intersection moment' of the timeless and time, is renewed in the order of nature in the recurring course of the seasons. And just as in the order of nature there takes place a 'magnifying of each its kind', both literally in 'sizing' and metaphorically in feeling 'with delight': so in the order of grace Mary calls to mind, and we with her, 'How she did in her stored / Magnify her Lord'. This notion is further elaborated by Hopkins in his other Marian poem, *The Blessed Virgin compared to the Air we Breathe*, where he speaks of the Incarnate Word of God, recalling how 'Of her flesh he took flesh' at Nazareth, and how in us, too, 'He does take fresh and fresh'—no longer in nature, but in spirit.

This might well seem a sufficient reason for 'offering Mary May'; but the poet has 'more than this'. It is, in fact, from this point that he rises to an enthusiastic crescendo with another, even more detailed depiction of the countryside in May. From his opening words he clearly hints at the climax to come, as he conveys an inscape of apple-blossom in the orchard with the characteristic epithet of 'drop-of-blood-and-foam-dapple' for the bloom that 'lights the orchard-apple'. He admires what he elsewhere calls 'earth's dapple' as it appears on the blossom, whose snow-white petals are flecked with crimson stains of blood—not any blood, but (as he explains in *Rosa Mystica*) the precious blood of Christ shed for our salvation. The blossom, he says, 'lights' *on* the branches ever so gracefully, like a bird of paradise, and at the same time lights them *up* with a new, almost supernatural illumination. He also rejoices to see in 'thicket and thorp'—in the villages and their surrounding clumps of trees—the 'silver-surfèd cherry', with its blossom floating on the branches like silvery surf on the waves of the sea.

Below the trees he conceives a yet deeper delight as he rests his eye on what seem lakes of bluebells. Possibly they were the same bluebells he had noted in his Journal during his previous residence at Stonyhurst in 1871, 'in the little wood between the College and the highroad and in one of the Hurst Green cloughs'. Then, too, he had noted how 'they came in falls of sky-colour washing the brows and slacks of the ground with vein-blue', making him exclaim, 'It was a lovely sight.' Similarly, on another occasion recorded in the Journal in the previous year, he had remarked of an individual bluebell: 'I do not think I have ever seen anything more beautiful . . . I know the beauty of Our Lord by it.' Thus, it is the bluebell among flowers, like the thrush among birds, that figures most prominently both in his poems and in the pages of his Journal.

Here, however, he prefers the name 'greybell' to 'bluebell'. Not that he is speaking of a different flower, but that he wishes to convey the precise impression both of the individual flower and of its multiple appearance in the wood. In its individuality it has a greyish hue that is gradually 'azuring over', no doubt, from the 'descending blue' of the sky. In its multiplicity the mixture of bluebells with a white variety gives a light greyish effect in itself; while in its scattered profusion over the grass it seems to be (transitively) 'azuring over' the ground. Thus it seems to wash the 'banks and brakes' of the woodland, not merely juxtaposing lakes and trees as in Wordsworth's poem on the daffodils, but positively merging the one into the other. Another reason for the choice of 'greybell' is the important consideration of sound: in that the 'g' of 'greybell' harmonizes better with the 'k' of 'banks and brakes' as well as 'lakes'; while the vowel in 'grey-' aptly echoes the similar vowel in 'azuring'.

Then from the 'banks and brakes'—with a reminiscence of Robert Burns and the 'banks and braes o' bonnie Doon'—the poet turns his attention to the chanting of little birds in the trees. What most engages his attention, however, is not the song of the thrush, as in *Spring*, or the score of the skylark in *The Sea and the Skylark*, but the magic call of the cuckoo. Here he seems to recall the other poem of Wordsworth on the cuckoo, with emphasis not so much on the bird as on its voice—'a wandering voice'. He also recalls an earlier passage from his Stonyhurst Journal for 1873, where he speaks of hearing 'the cuckoo with wonderful clear and plump and fluty notes', and goes on to describe how 'the hollow of a rising ground conceives them and palms them up and throws them out, like blowing into a big humming ewer'. He locates the sound 'under Saddle Hill one beautiful day and another time from Hodder wood'. This experience is caught in one of his unfinished poems, where he defines the call of the cuckoo as

> a ballad, a rebound
> Off trundled timber and scoops of the hillside ground, hollow
> hollow, hollow ground:
> The whole landscape flushes on a sudden at a sound.

Here, too, it is the sound of the cuckoo's voice which brings his poem on May to a climax, as it 'Caps, clears, and clinches all'.

Thus for the poet May is not just a month of brightness and delight, of flowers and renewed life. It is, more precisely, the month of motherhood with its ecstasy that a child is born into the world. As it fills with ecstasy all things on the face of mother earth, so it recalls the ecstatic memory of Mary when she gave birth to Christ her Saviour. Or rather, it recalls her ecstasy not so much in giving birth, which was at Bethlehem in the dead of winter, as during the time she bore him in her virginal womb, his 'Warm-laid grave of a womb-life grey'. During this time she carried him about in secret, removed from the curious gaze of the 'bent world', and she was filled with a 'mirth' she had there of her own, prompting her to utter her canticle of the Magnificat in response to her cousin Elizabeth's greeting. Then it was she broke out with words of praise and exultation 'In God who was her salvation'; and the words she uttered then are, for the poet, at the heart of what happens every year in Maytime.

By way of postscript, it is to this comforting thought that the poet significantly returns in the last year of his life, in the early spring of 1889, during the composition of his 'dark' sonnets in Dublin. Now he is in Ireland; now he is 'at a third / Remove'— from family, from friends, and from native country, which is for him as 'wife / To my creating thought'. Now he feels as it were 'Time's eunuch', who cannot 'breed one work that wakes'. Within himself he finds a 'winter world', which lacks 'The roll, the rise, the carol, the creation' of his earlier 'bright' sonnets.

> Thou art indeed just, Lord, if I contend
> With thee; but, sir, so what I plead is just.
> Why do sinners' ways prosper? and why must
> Disappointment all I endeavour end?
>
> Wert thou my enemy, O thou my friend,
> How wouldst thou worse, I wonder, than thou dost
> Defeat, thwart me? Oh, the sots and thralls of lust
> Do in spare hours more thrive than I that spend,
>
> Sir, life upon thy cause.

In the world outside he sees on the contrary

Banks and Brakes

banks and brakes
Now, leavèd how thick! lacèd they are again
With fretty chervil, look, and fresh wind shakes

Them; birds build—

But this only reminds him of his barren plight, as he continues with the
Miltonic lament from *Paradise Lost*: 'But not I build; no, but strain'.

All the same, in these lines of fond reminiscence at the dark end of his
life we sense the influence of his bright poems from the past, and of his
May Magnificat in particular. We also glimpse the smile of God breaking
on him unforeseen and, 'as skies / Betweenpie mountains', lighting 'a
lovely mile'. This memory alone serves him as his answer to the echo of
Jeremiah with which he begins his poem, and to his cries which he
compares in another 'dark' sonnet to

dead letters sent
To dearest him that lives alas! away.

The cries and the questions seem to fade away with his description of the
leafy 'banks and brakes' in spring-time, and of the 'fretty chervil' with its
delicate tracery of green leaves and white flowers shaking in the wind.
He returns indeed to his initial lament, recalling the 'strain' of his fruitless
life; but he does not remain on this mournful theme. Rather, he looks
up from himself to Christ, the 'lord of life', with the prayer: 'Send my
roots rain'—a prayer that not only rises out of the winter of desolation
within him, but is also suggested by the consolation of spring around
him. It may further be compared with the prayer with which he ends his
other poem, *The Blessed Virgin compared to the Air we Breathe*:

Worldmothering air, air wild,
Wound with thee, in thee isled,
Fold home, fast fold thy child.

8

My Aspens Dear

My aspens dear, whose airy cages quelled,
Quelled or quenched in leaves the leaping sun,
All felled, felled, are all felled;
 Of a fresh and following folded rank
  Not spared, not one
  That dandled a sandalled
  Shadow that swam or sank
On meadow and river and wind-wandering
     weed-winding bank.

 O if we but knew what we do
  When we delve or hew—
 Hack and rack the growing green!
  Since country is so tender
 To touch, her being só slender,
 That, like this sleek and seeing ball
 But a prick will make no eye at all,
 Where we, even where we mean
  To mend her we end her,
  When we hew or delve:
After-comers cannot guess the beauty been.
 Ten or twelve, only ten or twelve
  Strokes of havoc únselve
  The sweet especial scene,
  Rural scene, a rural scene,
  Sweet especial rural scene.

Binsey Poplars

In his love of nature Hopkins rests his delighted gaze as much on trees in
their various kinds as on wild flowers. He admires the loveliness of

bluebells and knows the beauty of Our Lord by them. But for trees he has a kind of fellow-feeling that amounts to love, particularly in a tragic context, as when he laments the fall of 'My aspens dear' in *Binsey Poplars*.

The variety of trees mentioned in his poems is indeed impressive. It is not just that he mentions them specifically by name; but whenever he mentions their name, he feels impelled to attach an appropriate epithet. Thus, in alphabetical order, he characterizes the abele (or white poplar) as 'airy'; the apple in bloom as 'drop-of-blood-and-foam-dapple'; the ash as 'scrolled', and the mountain ash (or rowan) as 'beadbonny'; the aspen as having 'airy cages'; the beech as 'silk'; the cherry in bloom as 'silver-surfèd'; the elm as 'arching', and the wych elm as 'wild'; the hazel as 'dogeared'; the hornbeam as 'fretty' (like chervil); the peartree as 'glassy'; the sallow as 'mealed-with-yellow'; the sycamore as 'packed'; and the whitebeam as 'windbeat'. In more general terms he delights in the thought of 'some sweet wood', or (with more detail) of 'some branchy bunchy bushybowered wood . . . That leans along the loins of hills'. On the other hand, he sees an ominous significance in the 'worlds of wanwood' that 'leafmeal lie' after summer, and in the 'beakleaved boughs dragonish' that 'damask the tool-smooth bleak light' after sunset.

This identification with trees, shimmering through other poems, is expressed in its most concentrated form in an unfinished poem, *Ashboughs*. 'Not of all my eyes see, wandering on the world,' the poet begins, with a combined echo of Milton and *Piers Plowman*,

> Is anything a milk to the mind so, so sighs deep
> Poetry tó it, as a tree whose boughs break in the sky.

Then he goes on to identify the species of tree he has in mind: 'Say it is áshboughs'. The delight he feels in them is no less in winter than in spring:

> whether on a December day and furled
> Fast ór they in clammyish lashtender combs creep
> Apart wide and new-nestle at heaven most high.

> They touch heaven, tabour on it; how their talons sweep
> The smouldering enormous winter welkin! May
> Mells blue and snowwhite through them, a fringe and fray
> Of greenery:

Such deep, almost personal love for trees is accompanied with bitter mourning and a sense of bereavement when they are, in any way or for any reason, maimed or felled—especially when deliberately so by human hands. Already while a scholastic studying philosophy at Stonyhurst, he had made the laconic note in his Journal for 1872: 'At the beginning of March they were felling some of the ashes in our grove.' But in the following year, after noting a similar occurrence, 'The ashtree growing in the corner of the garden was felled', he can no longer refrain from uttering his emotion: 'It was lopped first: I heard the sound and looking out and seeing it maimed there came at that moment a great pang and I wished to die and not to see the inscapes of the world destroyed any more.'

This is the feeling he recalls when, six years later, he returned to his *alma mater* of Oxford as a curate on the staff of St Aloysius' Church. In a poem written at that time he describes the place with growing enthusiasm as

Towery city and branchy between towers;
Cuckoo-echoing, bell-swarmèd, lark-charmèd, rook-racked, river-rounded;

But the beauty of the university city does not 'find him' so much as that of the nearby village of Binsey, with its characteristic row of black poplars lining the river-bank. Here in the Trinity term students would indulge in yachting along the curving river, or in the Hilary term in skating on the flooded, frozen expanse of the Port Meadow on its left bank. But here for some reason the poplars had recently been 'felled'; and the spectacle of devastation that now met his eyes on his return in early 1879 filled him not only with responsive sadness but also with poetic inspiration to compose a dirge or *threnos* over them.

In the title of his poem he names the trees 'Binsey Poplars', as if to designate the particular species associated in his affections with the village of Binsey. Between the component words of the name there is, moreover, a rough alliterative connection between 'B' and 'P', 'n' and 'l', as well as the two 's's. But in the opening words of the poem he prefers the more poetic name of 'aspens', partly for the sake of variety, partly to distinguish these poplars from the white poplars, or 'airy abeles', mentioned in *The Starlight Night*. More precisely, he may be referring to the *populus tremula*, which with its slender form and tremulous leaves forms a distinct species from either the white or the black poplar. But more probably he is using the name of 'aspen' (as it is not infrequently used) less precisely of the black poplar, which still in fact lines the river-bank by the Port Meadow.

From the first he speaks of these trees with a deep personal affection as 'My aspens dear'—as if they belonged to him by reason of their dearness to him. In the same way he speaks of the composer Henry Purcell, in

64

another Oxford poem of this year, as 'so dear to me'. In each case there is
pity mingled with affection in his feeling; and this he explains in his later
sonnet *Felix Randal*: it is 'This seeing the sick', who have fallen into a
pitiful condition, that 'endears them to us'—and, he adds, 'us too it
endears'. But first he recalls the living inscape of the aspens, like that of
the 'ashboughs', before going on to describe their present condition that
has evoked his pity.

It was formerly his delight, as with the 'glassy peartree' in *Spring*, to
look up from the river path at their branches against the blue sky—
whether 'furled' in winter, or 'apart wide' in a 'big wind' so that they
seem to 'touch heaven, tabour on it'. The branches he recalls as 'airy
cages' which, as they moved in the wind, seemed to imprison within their
leaves 'the leaping sun' like a wild creature in a zoo. More precisely, they
seemed to 'quell' the sun's impetuosity and to 'quench' its ardour for the
benefit of the passerby on a hot day in summer, thus earning his
gratitude. At the same time, there is in these two verbs a somewhat
ominous association; for though they are here used actively with 'the
leaping sun' as object, there is an implication (in the context) of passivity
with the 'aspens' themselves as subject. The association of 'quelled' soon
appears in its assonance with 'felled'; while that of 'quenched' is derived
from its echo of Othello's tragic soliloquy: 'If I quench thee, thou
flaming minister . . .' The relevance of this echo here is indicated by
Hopkins's use of it in two other poems: in *That Nature is a Heraclitean
Fire*, where he speaks of 'her bonniest, dearest to her, her clearest-selvèd
spark / Man' as quenched by death; and in *St Winefred's Well*, where
Caradoc with hands newly stained by the murder of Winefred asks in
despair, 'cómfort whére can I find / When 'ts light I quenched?'

So the poet proceeds to pour out his lament, with the sound of his
words aptly expressing their sense: 'All felled, felled, are all felled'. Here
the repetition of 'all' and 'felled' is particularly effective, as if he is not
only sighing deeply, but sobbing his heart out. It is significantly to this
pattern of words that he returns—though in the optative mood of
hope—in the opening line of *Henry Purcell*: 'Have fair fallen, O fair, fair
have fallen', where the heaviness of 'fallen' is relieved by the lightness of
'fair'. But here is no such relief. The heaviness of 'fallen' is only increased
by the accompanying repetition of 'all'. Hopkins is grieving with a
deeper grief than Margaret 'Over Goldengrove unleaving'; since her
grief was for a fall in the course of nature, but his is for a fall contrary to
nature—a stroke dealt by 'dear and dogged man' who, as he complains in
Ribblesdale, must 'reave our rich round world bare / And none reck of
world after'.

From his lament he returns to the memory of the poplars as ranged in 'a fresh and following folded rank' by the side of the river—perhaps recalling Celia's description of 'the rank of osiers by the murmuring stream' near her forest home in *As You Like It*. Here 'fresh' implies the freshness of the aspen leaves in early May; as for 'following', it evidently goes with 'rank', referring to the long line of trees planted by the riverside. But 'folded' is not so clear. It may refer to the overlapping outline of the aspen boughs as they reach outwards and upwards against the sky, or to the folded line of the trees as they are ranged along the river-bank. These epithets, with their initial 'f's and internal 'l's, all serve to echo the preceding 'fallen'; and they naturally occasion a fresh outbreak of grief, as the poet goes on: 'Not spared, not one.' Here, too, one may detect not one, but two Shakespearian echoes: from Macduff's lament over his murdered children, 'All my pretty ones? Did you say all? O hell-kite! All? What! all my pretty chickens and their dam, At one fell swoop?', and from Hamlet's first soliloquy, 'But two months dead: nay, not so much, not two.'

Then he turns once more from lament to reminiscence, picturing the poplars as children sitting by the river-bank and dandling their 'sandalled' feet in the water. The feet they dandle are their leafy boughs, whose shadows seem to swim or sink in the rippling river as they are lifted up and down by 'the bright wind boisterous'. The same shadows he sees ever rising and falling in the spring sunshine both on the 'wind-wandering weed-winding bank' and on the 'meadow' stretching out beyond. It is with this onomatopoeic description of the river and its bank, amplifying the 'fresh and following folded rank', that the poet concludes his first stanza on this tragic occasion.

In the second stanza he goes on to generalize his lamentation, and to involve the whole of man's fallen race—with an application of the dying words of the crucified Saviour: 'Father, forgive them: they know not what they do.' Only he rephrases these words in the form of an unfulfilled wish: 'If we only knew what we do'—with a possible memory of that other rephrasing by Claudio in *Much Ado About Nothing*: 'what men may do! what men daily do, not knowing what they do!' He deprecates the way men ill-treat the world of nature, when they 'delve or hew / Hack and rack the growing green'—just as in *Ribblesdale* he laments how man 'bids reel' the river and 'o'er gives all to rack or wrong'. He implies that in ill-treating it they are only unselving themselves—as he makes Caradoc realize after his murder of Winefred: 'I all my being have hacked in half with hér neck'. He contrasts their unfeeling recklessness with the tenderness of nature—'of a feathery delicacy' as of a maiden in her 'sweet being'.

He even compares the tenderness of nature to that of the human eye, regarding her as the apple of his own eye, which he calls 'this sleek and seeing ball'. He enforces the comparison by pointing out—with an echo of Hamlet's 'bare bodkin'—that 'But a prick will make no eye at all'. Here the pattern of metre and rhyme suggests a parallel—that extends from sound even to sense—with the couplet in *The Blessed Virgin compared to the Air we Breathe*, where the sun, without the protection of 'world-mothering air', is presented as

A blear and blinding ball
With blackness bound, and all.

In the next line there follows yet another echo from Hamlet's first soliloquy, 'Why she, even she', in the repetition of 'Where we, even where we mean / To mend her we end her.' The general sense is that of killing with too much kindness, or rather, with too much cruelty meant as kindness—in Hamlet's understanding of having to 'be cruel only to be kind'. Or as another of Shakespeare's characters remarks, in words that come closer to those of Hopkins, 'Striving to better, oft we mar what's well.' There is an implication that the trees have not been cut down from the roots, but have merely been thoroughly lopped or pollarded in the early spring. Anyhow, the sight they presented to Hopkins's eyes must have been a repulsive one, when he came across them in 1879 and compared them, first, with their former glory as he had known them in his student days, and then, with his previous experience of the felling of the ash-grove at Stonyhurst. Those who come after, he reflects, with no memory of their former glory and no experience of their tragic fall, 'cannot guess the beauty been'—the beauty of their 'sweet being in the beginning' when they seemed another 'Eden garden' on the banks of the Isis.

In this way the poet leads up to the climax in his conclusion, as he imagines the sound of the axe echoing in his ears—with the repeated 'ten or twelve, only ten or twelve / Strokes of havoc'. He does not say 'ten or eleven', nor 'eleven or twelve'. The monosyllabic 'ten' and 'twelve' are much more effective in suggesting the regular strokes of the axe hacking at the tree; while 'twelve' has the further, ominous rhyme with 'delve' and 'unselve'. He characterizes the strokes as 'strokes of havoc', with yet another echo from *Hamlet*, where Fortinbras, coming on the final scene of carnage, exclaims:

This quarry cries on havoc. O proud death!
What feast is toward in thine eternal cell?

The effect of the strokes is to 'unselve', that is, to unmake what has been bound in the strain and stress of being. In similar terms the poet describes the evening of life, in *Spelt from Sibyl's Leaves*, when 'earth her being has unbound, her dapple is at end', when self is 'ín self steepèd and páshed—qúite / Disremembering, dísmémbering áll now', and when 'selfwrung, selfstrung, sheathe- and shelterless, thóughts agaínst thoughts ín groans grínd.'

What is here unselved, the innocent victim of the slaughter, is 'The sweet especial scene' of Binsey Poplars. Before he called them 'dear', but now he uses 'sweet' as his favourite variant of 'dear', recalling 'the earth's sweet being' from *Spring* and foreshadowing the 'Earth, sweet earth, sweet landscape' of *Ribblesdale*. Similarly, 'especial' foreshadows the 'arch-especial a spirit' of *Henry Purcell*—with the prefix employed to separate 'sweet' from 'special' in sound and thus to soften the effect of the line. As for the sense, the scene is particularly 'especial' for its rural landscape and inscape, as forming a notable part of the 'Rural rural keeping' of *Duns Scotus's Oxford*. So the poet repeats the phrase, partly with childish delight in the sound of the words, but rather with mournful recollection of a scene that is no more. 'Rural scene, a rural scene'—where the addition of the indefinite article seems to imply an affirmation: '(Yes, it was) a rural scene.' Finally, he puts all three epithets together in a concluding affirmation: '(Yes, it was a) Sweet especial rural scene'; and thus he leaves it, though outwardly departed, deeply imprinted on the minds and memories of his readers.

9
Goldengrove Unleaving

to a young child

Márgarét, áre you gríeving
Over Goldengrove unleaving?
Léaves, líke the things of man, you
With your fresh thoughts care for, can you?
Áh! ás the heart grows older
It will come to such sights colder
By and by, nor spare a sigh
Though worlds of wanwood leafmeal lie;
And yet you *will* weep and know why.
Now no matter, child, the name:
Sórrow's spríngs áre the same.
Nor mouth had, no nor mind, expressed
What heart heard of, ghost guessed:
It ís the blight man was born for,
It is Margaret you mourn for.

Spring and Fall

In the development of Hopkins's poetic spirit there is a natural decline from morning to evening, from spring to autumn, from the joy of youth to the sadness of old age. The turning-point comes all too soon after the brief period of 'bright' sonnets dating from his *Wreck of the Deutschland* in 1876. So long as he remained in the surroundings of North Wales, devoted to the congenial studies of theology and Ignatian asceticism at St Beuno's College, his Muse rejoiced in a glad springtime. But after his ordination to the priesthood on 23 September, 1877, he found himself denied the extra year of theology he had been looking forward to and thrust into an active ministry to which he was little suited by temperament or by training. His first experiences of such ministry, at the

boarding-school of Mount St Mary's near Sheffield, and at the parish of
St Aloysius's in Oxford, were tolerable enough, though not without
complaint; and he continued to produce poems in continuation of his
first flush of enthusiasm at St Beuno's. But from the time he went north
in 1879, into the waste land of industrial Lancashire, his complaints
became more frequent and his enthusiasm was abated. He remained
happy enough at Bedford Leigh, where he spent a few months in parish
work from September to December, 1879; but in January of the following year he was appointed to the larger parish of St Francis Xavier's,
Liverpool, close to the heart of the dockyard slums. Soon after he wrote
to his friend, Canon Dixon: 'Liverpool is of all places the most museless.
It is indeed a most unhappy and miserable spot.'

Oddly enough, yet appropriately enough, it was here that Hopkins
composed one of his most charming and deservedly popular, yet one of
his saddest and most pessimistic poems, entitled *Spring and Fall*. In many
ways it reads like a continuation of *Binsey Poplars*, which he had recently
composed at Oxford, particularly in its lament for the passing of natural
beauty. But there is a deep difference: in that poem the stroke is dealt by
human carelessness and cruelty, whereas in this it is presented as part of
the unvarying round of the seasons. In both poems the theme of 'fall' is
prominent. But again there is a difference: in that poem it assumes the
passive form of the causative verb 'fell', where the aspens are lamented as
'All felled, felled, are all felled', whereas in this it takes the more static,
fatalistic form of the abstract noun 'Fall' in the title, whether this be
interpreted as the fall of leaves from the trees or the fall of the year in the
autumn. In both poems, too, the contemplation of this common theme
leads to lament. But once more there is a difference: in that poem the
lamenter is the poet himself, whereas in this it is the young child to
whom he addresses his words of sympathy and adult advice.

In a letter of 5 September, 1886, to Robert Bridges, in which he sends
his friend his first copy of the poem, Hopkins states that it was 'not
founded on any real incident', such as had inspired two other poems of
his that year, *Felix Randal* and *Brothers*. But it may well have been
written with a particular child in mind, a child with the haunting name
of Margaret—which would explain the unusual simplicity of its language. And it was certainly composed in early autumn, on the occasion
(as the poet told his friend Canon Dixon) of a walk from Lydiate to the
north of Liverpool, with the vague intention of having it set to
plainsong—which would explain the unusual regularity of its metre: in
iambic tetrameter with rhyming couplets. What is fictitious, however, is
the situation of the child grieving over the fallen leaves and the identification of the place as Goldengrove. Not that there is no such place. The

poet himself would have been familiar with the name, partly from his walks round St Beuno's, which might have taken him to a Goldengrove in Flintshire, partly from his probable reading of the popular seventeenth-century divine, Jeremy Taylor, who had named several of his works after the house in Carmarthenshire where he had composed them in peaceful retirement from the Civil War. But his choice of the name was determined, not by any actual place, but by the romantic associations of its sound with the Golden Age and with some enchanted grove.

He opens his poem with the haunting name of Margaret—evoking as it does the twofold meaning of 'pearl' (from the Latin *margarita*) and 'daisy' (from the French *marguerite*)—emphasizing it by two stresses, one on the first and the other on the last syllable. The 'g' and 'r' of the name look forward to the verb 'grieve'; while the vowel 'a' that unites them in one syllable looks forward to the progressive form of this verb, in the question: 'Are you gríeving?' Thus he passes from the grieving subject to the object of her grief, 'Goldengrove', along with the reason for her grief, 'unleaving'. Here in the opening couplet we are presented with the basic situation out of which the poem arises and in which it remains: the confrontation between 'Márgarét gríeving' and 'Goldengrove unleaving'. It is, moreover, emphasized all the more pointedly by the rhyme that holds them together, as it were in some archetypal relation that has been 'From life's dawn . . . drawn down' (*The Wreck of the Deutschland* stanza 20). It is partly, no doubt, this contrast which is indicated in the abstract ambiguity of the title. On the one hand, the child with her 'fresh thoughts' and her nominal association with pearls and daisies may be said to represent the spring of life, or what the poet calls in his sonnet on *Spring* 'Innocent mind and Mayday in girl and boy'. On the other hand, the 'unleaving' trees of Goldengrove, for all their nostalgic evocation of a Golden Age (or rather because of it), may be seen as representing what the poet elsewhere calls 'the year's fall' (in *The Wreck* stanza 32). But in the course of the poem another, more fundamental reason for the title becomes apparent.

The child's grief over the fallen leaves may seem a case of 'the pathetic fallacy', and in the poet's sympathy with her some critics have found an unpleasing sentimentality over the 'passing of all mortal things'. Yet in her instinctive grief, and in his more knowing grief, there is depth upon depth of meaning, which when rightly understood effectively removes this superficial impression of sentimentality. From the mention of 'leaves' the poet passes on immediately to a comparison with 'the things of man'—echoing the *mortalia* of Virgil's famous line in the *Aeneid*: '*Sunt lacrimae rerum et mentem mortalia tangunt*'. He goes on to express his

71

astonishment, not unmixed with admiration, at the metaphysical manner in which the child with her 'fresh thoughts' can care for the fallen leaves. He then turns his astonishment into a rhetorical question, with the addition of 'can you?'—which not only completes the rhyme of the couplet, but also evokes the series of similar questions in *The Wreck* (stanza 18), whose poetic effect is much the same:

> Ah, touched in your bower of bone,
> Are you! turned for an exquisite smart,
> Have you! make words break from me here all alone,
> Do you!

It is possibly this evocation which prompts the exclamation 'Ah!' at the head of the following line. There is a deep meaning in this sigh: the meaning developed by Wordsworth in his *Ode to Immortality* as he traced human growth from the 'visionary gleam' of childhood through the 'Shades of the prison-house' that 'close / Upon the growing boy' to the 'light of common day' into which the vision fades in manhood. For a Romantic poet like Hopkins, writing within this Wordsworthian tradition, the tragedy of man's earthly existence is precisely that 'the heart grows older' and that custom (as Wordsworth continues) comes to lie upon it 'with a weight / Heavy as frost, and deep almost as life'. This mention of 'frost' in connection with 'custom' may perhaps have prompted Hopkins's rhyme of 'older' with 'colder'. It is only the young in heart, he sadly reflects, who weep over the fallen leaves of autumn: as the heart grows older, it becomes accustomed to such sights and views them coldly without feeling.

There is something Elizabethan, and particularly Shakespearian, about the lament for the golden days of the past implied in 'nor spare a sigh' in the next line—with its sibilant echo of 'by and by'. It evokes the same feeling as Feste's melancholy song in *Twelfth Night*, 'Come away, come away, Death'—especially the line, 'A thousand thousand sighs to save'. It also recalls the plaintive conclusion of *The Phoenix and the Turtle*: 'For these dead birds sigh a prayer.' Such sighing for the past is indeed negated by those who have become colder to such sights; but the poet's lament is sufficient proof that he does not participate in their negation. Rather, he is led by his sympathetic feeling to the most poetic line of his poem: 'Though worlds of wanwood leafmeal lie'—an inspired alteration of his original draft: 'Though forests low and leafmeal lie'. He has preserved the alliterative 'leafmeal lie', with its coined application of 'piecemeal' to leaves of autumn; and he has replaced the colourless 'forests' with the finely alliterative 'worlds of wanwood', another coinage in which the

Old English 'wan' (as negative prefix), or archaic 'wan' (pale), or obsolete 'wan' (gloomy), is coupled with the common 'wood' to produce something rich and strange.

Yet even if she comes in adulthood 'to such sights colder', he tells the child, she will have ample cause to bemoan her human, or womanly, condition—not perhaps at the sight of fallen leaves, but at what they actually symbolize in human life. Then she will know the reason why she is weeping, though it may be less fundamental and less mystical than that which now causes her to grieve. For the time being, however, ignorance is bliss; nor is it expedient for him to tell her beforehand of the griefs that will come to oppress her in adulthood. Even if he named them, they would mean nothing to her innocent mind. In any case, the springs of sorrow, though apparently different for children and for adults, are all fundamentally the same: the original separation of creatures from their Creator, which antedates and underlies all human memory. Here we come to the deeper, theological significance of the title, *Spring and Fall*. The former word may well mean a spring of tears, or rather, the ultimate spring of human sorrow, which is elsewhere mentioned by the poet as 'a chief woe, world-sorrow'. The latter word, in apposition to the former, would then refer to the Fall of Man, by his rejection of obedience to God, which is the spring of all his subsequent sorrows.

This spring, the poet continues, is a tragedy of human life and human origin that no mouth has ever adequately expressed, nor mind ever aptly conceived. Here he seems to reverse the application of Isaiah's similar words to the joys of heaven, which 'eye hath not seen, nor ear heard, neither hath it entered into the heart of man to conceive'. These words he has already echoed in their original sense in *The Wreck* (stanza 26): 'The treasure never eyesight got, nor was ever guessed what for the hearing?'. But in his reversed application of them to the sorrows of earth, he only goes half-way. What he says is that, whereas 'Nor mouth had, no nor mind, expressed', yet 'heart heard of, ghost guessed' the truth: the negative is followed by an affirmative. For some inkling of the fundamental reason of human grief has indeed reached, if not the rational mind of man, his masculine *animus*, at least the instinctive heart, his feminine *anima*. It is the heart, as the poet points out in *The Wreck* (stanza 18), which is the 'mother of being' in man, and which, though 'unteachably after evil', yet utters the truth out of a reason which (in Pascal's famous words) the reason does not recognize. This is (to use an old-fashioned word) the 'ghost' or inmost spirit of man—what medieval philosophers called the *synderesis animae*, with its *potentia obedientialis*. It is here, in the deepest heart of man, that the spring of sorrow is most keenly felt, as he confesses his guilt and is melted to tears of repentance.

Such then, the poet concludes, is the blight of original sin in which man is born into the world, and for which he has to pay the penalty every day of his mortal life. As a medieval poet put it, in words which his Victorian successor may be consciously echoing,

Lollai litel child, whi wepistow so sore?
Nedis mostou wepe, hit was iyarkid the yore.

It is a blight so intrinsic to human nature and to each human individual, that the poet can even conclude: not just 'It is Man you mourn for', but more precisely 'It is Margaret you mourn for'. Growing old is, as Newman sadly remarked, 'a process of unlearning life's poetry and learning its prose'. There is an intimate connection between this condition of sinners on earth and that of the damned in hell, whose spring of sorrow is precisely (as he remarks in the darkest of his dark sonnets) to be 'their sweating selves': they are their own blight and bane. On this pessimistic note he brings his poem to an end—though it is not unique in such an ending, even at this period of his career. Its whole movement, for all its graceful simplicity, is from joy to sadness, from the freshness of youth to the sadness of old age, in a word, from Spring to Fall. It is only rendered endurable by the fact that the poet himself, while lamenting the Fall of Man, keeps his own thoughts as fresh as those of the child he is addressing.

10

This Darksome Burn

This darksome burn, horseback brown,
His rollrock highroad roaring down,
In coop and in comb the fleece of his foam
Flutes and low to the lake falls home.

A windpuff-bonnet of fáwn-fróth
Turns and twindles over the broth
Of a pool so pitchblack, féll-fró wning,
It rounds and rounds Despair to drowning.

Degged with dew, dappled with dew
Are the groins of the braes that the brook treads through,
Wiry heathpacks, flitches of fern,
And the beadbonny ash that sits over the burn.

What would the world be, once bereft
Of wet and of wilderness? Let them be left,
O let them be left, wildness and wet;
Long live the weeds and the wilderness yet.

Inversnaid

Among all Hopkins's poems there is something unique about *Inversnaid*. In the first place, whereas his other poems draw inspiration from the scenery of England and Wales, and even of Ireland, this is his only poem that represents the more romantic scenery of Scotland. In itself, the poem is a fine example of his delight in natural inscape and of his skilful use of sprung rhythm to reinforce his verbal description. It is also his one extended treatment of a mountain stream, concentrating its various features in a single poetic inscape, and catching its cascading downward

75

movement in the rhythm. This is no chance effusion of the poet, standing by itself in isolation from his other poems. It is rather to be seen as the climax to a certain development which may be traced back to his early poems and fragments of his early diaries. From the beginning, for example in *The Alchemist in the City*, we find in Hopkins a deep love of wild places: 'But I desire the wilderness', and in an early fragment recorded in 1865: 'O what a silence is this wilderness!' More recently, in a letter to Bridges in 1879, he was projecting a poem on the decline of nature in the modern world, beginning with the plaintive question: 'Oh where is it, the wilderness, the wildness of the wilderness?' Now on his first visit to the Scottish Highlands in the summer of 1881, he found the fulfilment of his desire and the answer to his questionings at Inversnaid on Loch Lomond.

On the other hand, there is something apparently uncharacteristic of Hopkins in this poem, with its absence of theological reflection. It remains almost entirely on the level of nature, moving from three stanzas of natural description to a conclusion in which the poet makes an impassioned plea for the wildness of nature. Lacking as it does the theological dimension of his other poems, it seems to emphasize the Dionysian, rather than Apollonian, aspect of Hopkins's inspiration.

The keynote of the poem is struck in a later letter to his friend Baillie, describing the occasion of his visit to Loch Lomond, though without reference to his composition of the poem. 'The day was dark,' he says, 'and partly hid the lake, yet it did not altogether disfigure it but gave a pensive or solemn beauty which left a deep impression on me.' This is just the impression conveyed by *Inversnaid*. In spite of the mention of 'dappled' there is little sense of colour. At most, we have 'brown' and 'fawn', merging into 'darksome' and 'pitchblack', as contrasted with the whiteness of 'fleece' and the brightness of 'dew'. In this imagery Hopkins seems to be moving towards the stark contrast of 'black, white' in *Spelt from Sibyl's Leaves*. His attention is particularly arrested by the moving water of the stream and the 'wet' of its surroundings, whether from the spray of its falls or from the rain or drizzle so frequent a feature of mountainous climate. He thus imparts to his poem an impression of monochrome, without declining into monotony. If anything, the words he chooses are more than usually charged with meaning; so that for a full appreciation of the poem one has to be keenly aware of every implication and ambiguity and association in sense and in sound, without losing sight of the total meaning.

In the opening stanza the poet presents a general view of the burn, Arklet Water, as it flows down from Loch Arklet among the Trossachs and enters Loch Lomond near the hamlet of Inversnaid. In the first word he lays emphasis on the *haecceitas*, or 'this-ness', of the burn, before going on to communicate its inscape by means of descriptive words. We may note a contrast between the opening 'this' of this poem and the concluding 'this' of *The Soldier*, where it receives a full and final stress. The stream is designated in Scottish idiom as 'burn', as in Bannockburn—with a possible suggestion of the name of the Scottish national poet, Robert Burns, whose songs are echoed lower down. The connection between 'burn' and 'brown' in the first line is also etymological, the adjective being derived from Old English 'brun' and the cognate verb 'to burn'. In the 'darksome' appearance of the burn there is at once something attractive, as in 'darksome darksome Penmaen Pool' of that earlier poem, and something threatening, as in the 'darksome devouring eyes' of *Carrion Comfort*. Both qualities are drawn out more explicitly in the course of the poem.

Then the power of the water rushing down the slope reminds the poet of a galloping horse. At the same time, the compound 'horseback' is suggestive of the switchback and the merry-go-round at a fair, in conjunction with the words that follow: 'rollrock', 'twindles', 'pitch-black' and 'flitches'. In this context the colour of the stream is no ordinary brown, but the glossy brown of a horse's hide, which characterizes the water in much the same way as in *Epithalamion*:

> where a gluegold-brown
> Marbled river, boisterously beautiful, between
> Roots and rocks is danced and dandled, all in froth and water-blowballs, down.

Similarly, in his Journal for 1873, Hopkins describes the colour of the water at Hodder Roughs as 'velvety brown like ginger syrop'.

Continuing the metaphor, the poet presents the burn as it rolls rocks downstream in terms of a horse-cart rolling from side to side and rocking forwards and backwards in full career. He conceives it as a horse galloping down the highroad, until it comes to the obstacles detailed in the third stanza, when it has to 'tread' more carefully. In its loud movement 'roaring down' it contains a suggestion of wild, even monstrous nature, as in 'Night roared' in *The Wreck of the Deutschland*; so that the horse comes to take on the terrible features of the lion in *Carrion Comfort*.

The places past which, or over which, the water rushes headlong, are variously identified as 'coop' and 'comb'. In the former the water is cooped in by rocks and is forced to flow through with even greater rapidity. The word itself suggests the verb 'scoop', as used by Hopkins in his Journal for 1873: 'Round holes are scooped in the rocks smooth and true like turning: they look like the hollow of a vault or bowl'; and also the adjective 'scuppled', as used in his Journal of the same year: 'I saw big smooth flinty waves, carved and scuppled in shallow grooves'. In the latter the water flows over the rocks with a ribbed or 'roping' effect, as described in the same Journal: 'making a bold big white bow coiling its edge over and splaying into ribs', and with 'heavy locks or brushes like shaggy rope-ends rolling down from a corner of the falls and one huddling over another'. It is precisely this effect which is sketched by the poet in his drawing of 'The Baths of Rosenlaui' in 1868.

The torrential foam of the water as it encounters various obstacles in its course Hopkins characteristically compares to white fleece—as in *The Wreck of the Deutschland*: 'the cobbled foam-fleece'. He also describes it in connection with Hodder Roughs (which evidently enter into his perception of Inversnaid) in his Journal: 'Below the rock the bubble-jestled skirt of foam jumping back against the fall.'

Further metaphors are packed into the next line. 'Flutes' is primarily an architectural metaphor from the fluting on pillars; and as such it suggests the shape and movement of the water as it ropes over or flows in narrow channels between the rocks. But it may also contain a secondary association with the sound of a flute, in a musical metaphor. There is an air of suspense in this word, as it continues the sense from the previous line only to be broken by the conjunction 'and'. The following adjective 'low' further suggests the exclamation 'lo!' One imagines the poet looking down the waterfall to where the stream at last joins the lake. Here he changes the metaphor, comparing the water as it reaches its place of rest to a homing pigeon arriving at its destination. It is a metaphor frequently repeated by Hopkins, as in *The Handsome Heart* where he compares 'homing nature' to 'carriers let fly'.

In the next stanza he depicts a particular scene along the burn—a dark pool through which it passes on its way to the lake. He directs his attention to the foam on the surface of the water, which he characterizes as 'windpuff-bonnet of fáwn-fróth'. There are similar word-patterns in *That Nature is a Heraclitean Fire*, where he speaks of 'Cloud-puffball, torn tufts' with reference to cloud formations in the sky, and in *Epithalamion*, where he refers to 'froth and water-blowballs' on the water (as here). The foam or froth, puffed by the wind, has a fawn colour, with a suggestion of the delicacy and timidity of a fawn. To express its movement he uses a portmanteau word of his own coinage: 'twindles', which combines 'twitches' and 'dwindles', as the froth is blown about and forms into smaller bubbles. The sense of this word may be illustrated from two passages of the Journal for 1872: 'The foam dwindling and twitched into long chains of suds', and 'It is broken small and so unfolding till it runs in threads and thrums twitching down the backdraught to the sea again'.

Coming to the pool, the poet envisages it as a witches' cauldron over a fire, with broth coming to the boil. His imagination of hell is reinforced by the adjective 'pitchblack', associated as it is with the pool of fire or lower pit of the Gospels and *Book of Revelation*. 'Fell', too, rhymes with hell; and 'frowning' recalls the passage on hell in *The Wreck of the Deutschland*: 'The frown of his face / Before me, the hurtle of hell / Behind'. In its first meaning, 'fell' is, of course, an adjective meaning cruel, and used adverbially with 'frowning'. There is a parallel in the words of Fury in the 'dark' sonnet *No worst*: 'Let me be fell'. But it may also contain the sense of 'fall' in the past tense (with its theological implications), the connection with a 'fell' or mountain, and even the 'fell' or skin of a wild beast—seeing how closely all these words and meanings are associated in Hopkins's mind.

The pool itself moves round and round in a perpetual eddy or whirlpool, or rather it makes the froth on its surface move round. In a kind of pathetic fallacy, the poet sees the froth as a personification of Despair—in an allegorization which we also find in *Carrion Comfort* and *The Wreck of the Deutschland*. At the same time, 'rounds' may be taken in its secondary sense of whispers—from Old English 'runian'. In this case, Despair may be either the indirect object, the person to whom the pool is whispering, or the direct object, the word spoken by the pool to the froth—as in *The Leaden Echo*: 'Despair, despair, despair, despair.' Finally, the froth disappears and drowns in the pool, as the dark climax of the stanza. But it leaves another, more hopeful meaning possible. For if Despair drowns, in the image of froth, then it gives place to Hope: just as the 'leaden echo' gives place to the 'golden echo'.

In contrast to the darkness of the pool, the banks on either side are shown in the third stanza glistening with wet drops that reflect a brightness in the air. In describing them as 'degged with dew', the poet is drawing on a Lancashire dialect word meaning sprinkled—as in 'degging-can' for watering-can. It contains a convenient alliteration with 'dew', and a suggestion of the 'down-dugged ground-hugged grey' of the mist in *The Wreck of the Deutschland*, besides reinforcing a rhythmical parallel with 'Trenched with tears, carved with cares' in that poem. He repeats the word 'dew' in further connection with a favourite inscape-word, 'dappled', used here to indicate not a variety of colour, but a difference of light and shade on rock and heather, on fern and ash.

As for the banks themselves, their description as 'groins' brings in a combined architectural and bodily metaphor: the former referring to the joints of vaulting in an arched roof, and the latter to the joining of the legs in the human body. A similar use of the latter metaphor recurs in *Epithalamion*, where a wood is said to lean 'along the loins of hills'. The banks are termed 'braes', which have the implication of steepness, besides an association with Burns's well-known songs, *Ye banks and braes o' bonny Doon* and *By yon bonny banks and by yon bonny braes*. The stream itself is now termed 'the brook', as if in reminiscence of Tennyson's poem of that title. In contrast to its former roaring, it now has to 'tread' its way carefully among the rocks, and to thread its way through them. There is a heavy feeling in 'tread', as in *The Wreck of the Deutschland*, 'trod hard down', in *God's Grandeur*, 'Generations have trod, have trod, have trod', and in *The Golden Echo*, 'O then, weary then whý should we tread?'

There follows a detailed sketch of the plants growing on either side of the brook. 'Wiry heathpacks' are clumps of heather, packed densely together, with rough, wiry stalks. The 'flitches of fern' (defined in the OED as strips or slices cut from a tree) is another portmanteau word, suggesting the movement of fern as it twitches, flinches and switches back after being flicked or brushed aside by a passer-by. The 'beadbonny ash' is variously reflected in the Journal, where Hopkins speaks of the 'skeleton inscape of a spray-end of ash' with a 'suggested globe', of 'a heap of fruity purplish anthers looking something like unripe elderberries', or ashes whose 'combs are not wiry and straight but rich and beautifully curled'. But here he is probably referring not to the ash, but to the rowan or mountain-ash, with its beaded orange berries. 'Bead' may also refer to beads of dew; while 'bonny' recalls the two songs of Burns mentioned above. The tree is described as growing out over the burn, possibly with a bough curving out and upwards, on which one might sit above the water. In the association of 'ash' and 'burn', moreover, there is a probable pun, recalling the 'blue-bleak embers' of *The Windhover* and the 'world's wildfire' that leaves 'but ash' in *That Nature is a Heraclitean Fire*.

Finally, the poet concludes with a plea for the preservation of nature with all its wildness and its wet. He thus extends his thought from this particular scene to the whole world—not just the physical world of nature, but the moral world of man as well, considering that man is (as he points out in *Ribblesdale*) 'Earth's eye, tongue, or heart'. The world, he reflects, is always being spoiled by the 'selfbent' of 'dear and dogged man'; but it is just as always revived by the 'dearest freshness' proceeding from the Holy Ghost. He sees wildness as essential to the world's being, even such wildness as he has discovered in the impressive scenery of the Scottish Highlands in rainy or misty weather. And through the wildness of nature he looks to something wild and untamed in the human heart,

Upper falls of Inversnaid
Below The horseback brown of the burn

Lower falls of Inversnaid
Below The beadbonny ash, or rowantree

The groins of the braes
Below Heathpacks and gorse on the braes
Overleaf Rowan and flitches of fern at the top of the burn

Yellow hornlight over St Beuno's
Below The same with hollow hoarlight

Earnest, earthless, equal, attuneable, vaulty, voluminous, ... stupend
Evening strains to be time's ... vast, womb-of-all, home-of-all, hearse-

Her fond yellow hornlight low with the west and the cold hoar
-all, hearse-of-all night,
hoarlight following the height
Waste, and the earliest stars, earlstars, principal light; and
Fire-featuring heaven

Her fond yellow hornlight wound to the west, her wild hollow
hoarlight hung to the height   [read as
Waste and her earliest stars, earlstars, stars principal, over
Firefeaturing heaven. For earth her being unbound; the day
is at an end, a

Stray, aswarm, throughther, in throngs; self
Stray and aswarm   self steeped in self, quite in her,
Dismembering, disremembering all.   quite

Swarm, swarms throughther, in throng; self she has in self steep
in her; quite (at right)
Dismembering, disremembering all.

Swarm, swarms, all throughther, in throng; self in self steep
and flush; quite right
Dismembering, disremembering all.

Evening strains to be time's-well, world's-pit, womb-of-
home-of-all, hearse-of-all night

An evening sky
Below Beakleaved boughs against the bleak light
Opposite Early draft manuscript of *Spelt from Sibyl's Leaves* in GMH's Dublin notebook

Portrait of a brother and sister

Monasterevan House
Below Burling barrow brown near Monasterevan

The Dry Dene of Holywell
Below Upper garden and Anglican church of Holywell

The Kentish Knock
Below Mount St Mary's, Derbyshire

Ventnor and Boniface Down, Isle of Wight
Below Carisbrooke Castle

Appledurcombe Manor
Below Appledurcombe Farm
Opposite Society of Jesus plot in Glasnevin cemetery

Left Detail of the window
Right Memorial window to Hopkins at St Bartholomew's, Haslemere

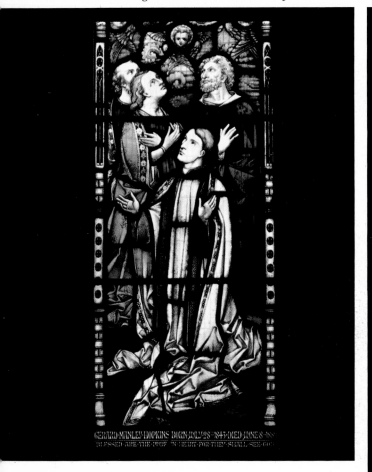

that 'homing nature . . . wild and self-instressed' of which he speaks in *The Handsome Heart*.

As for his complementary nostalgia for 'wet', its meaning and charm is repeated in his other phrase in *To what serves Mortal Beauty?*: 'wetfresh windfalls of war's storm'. It is associated in his mind with the 'dearest freshness deep down things' in the heart of nature, and with the description of Paradise in *Genesis* ii: 'But a spring rose out of the earth, watering all the surface of the earth' (Douai version). There is also a connection with 'weeds', which appears both in the last line of this poem, and in his sonnet on *Duns Scotus's Oxford*: 'These weeds and waters.' He thinks of weeds not as unwanted, but as wild flowers; and he hears in their sound an assonance with sweet, recalling 'A strain of the earth's sweet being in the beginning / In Eden garden'.

The poet's plea for the 'wildness and wet' of nature, twice repeated in his vehement desire, is simply: 'Let them be left'. As in *Ribblesdale*, he pleads on behalf of 'Earth, sweet earth', which has 'no tongue to plead, no heart to feel'. As in *God's Grandeur* and *The Sea and the Skylark*, he is jealous for the purity of nature against the sordid selfishness of man, whose hands are 'smeared with toil'. His repetition both of this plea and of its object suggests a musical refrain, analogous to that in *The Woodlark*, 'With a sweet joy of a sweet joy', that in *Binsey Poplars*, the 'sweet especial rural scene', and that in *Brothers*, 'Dearly thou canst be kind'. In each of these cases there is an emphasis on the sweetness or kindness at the heart of nature, which is for the poet the fundamental meaning of 'wildness and wet'.

Yet his plea is not a hopeless one. He looks not to the likelihood of ruin, but to the certainty of resurrection. In his poem as a whole there is a structural contrast between the downward fall of the stream, to the drowning of Despair at the end of the second stanza, and the upward rising of the banks on either side, sprinkled as they are with bright dew and looking up to the sky through the branches of the 'beadbonny ash'. This rising movement culminates in the 'long live' of the final line, which is not just a ceremonial *'Viva!'* or an outburst of forced enthusiasm, but the poet's confession of his faith in eternal life. Thus in the end of the poem we may discern theological undertones of Baptism and Resurrection, such as are developed more explicitly in *That Nature is a Heraclitean Fire*. It is significant that so many phrases from this poem are taken up in the latter: in 'cloud-puffball', in 'pool', in 'treadmire toil', in 'nature's bonfire burns on', in 'her bonniest', in 'in an enormous dark drowned', in 'world's wildfire' and 'leave but ash'. Through this connection between the two poems, it is possible to take what is explicit in the latter—especially its theology of death and life—so as to interpret what remains only implicit in the former.

81

11

Wild Hollow Hoarlight

Earnest, earthless, equal, attuneable, | vaulty, voluminous, . . . stupendous
Evening strains to be tíme's vást, | womb-of-all, home-of-all, hearse-of-
all night.
Her fond yellow hornlight wound to the west, | her wild hollow
hoarlight hung to the height
Waste; her earliest stars, earlstars, | stárs principal, overbend us,
Fíre-féaturing heaven. For earth | her being has unbound; her dapple is at
end, as—
tray or aswarm, all throughther, in throngs; | self ín self steepèd and
páshed—qúite
Disremembering, dísmémbering | áll now. Heart, you round me right
With: Óur évening is over us; óur night | whélms, whélms, ánd will end
us.
Only the beakleaved boughs dragonish | damask the tool-smooth bleak
light; black,
Ever so black on it. Óur tale, O óur oracle! | Lét life, wáned, ah lét life
wind
Off hér once skéined stained véined varíety | upon, áll on twó spools;
párt, pen, páck
Now her áll in twó flocks, twó folds—black, white; | right, wrong;
reckon but, reck but, mind
But thése two; wáre of a wórld where bút these | twó tell, each off the
óther; or a rack
Where, selfwrung, selfstrung, sheathe- and shelterless, | thóughts agaínst
thoughts ín groans grínd.

Spelt from Sibyl's Leaves

Hopkins is commonly thought of as the poet of 'pied beauty' and 'earth's
dapple', of the day and the spring-time, of an enthusiastic 'hurrahing' and

glorifying of 'God's grandeur'. He is indeed all that. But if he were only that, there would be something lacking in him, both as man and as poet, for that is only one side of human experience. There is another, darker side as well, the side which corresponds to the darkness of night and the desolation of winter, and which no poet can afford to neglect in his poetic view of man and nature. Hopkins does not try to ignore this side; nor does he commemorate it merely in passing. Rather, it forms no less important a part of his poetic *corpus* than the former side. If we have his 'bright' sonnets, we also have his 'dark'—even 'terrible'—sonnets to balance them, sonnets which may be said to rank among the darkest poems in English literature. He was never a poet of the plains, where all is flat and gentle, as in the English Midlands. He is rather a poet of mountains and valleys, as in the 'world of Wales' or among the Pennines near Stonyhurst. So if he has his heights of poetic enthusiasm and exultation, he has also his depths—no less poetically inspired—of despondency and depression, his

> cliffs of fall
> Frightful, sheer, no-man-fathomed.

His period of despondency we may date with reasonable accuracy from the day of his going from Stonyhurst to Dublin in the autumn of 1884. There he found himself, as he says, 'at a third remove' from his family, his friends, and his country. More than in the past his life there was 'among strangers', even stranger to him than the unkind 'inmates' of Wales. And somehow in this strange land, with its strange inscapes, or absence of inscape in Dublin, he found himself strangely deprived of poetic inspiration. Not that he was treated unkindly by the normally hospitable Irish; but he felt himself out of place among them, as an Englishman in a land whose people he could see were being unjustly treated by his own government. So he expresses himself 'wear- / y of idle a being but by where wars are rife'. In such an atmosphere—further darkened by his own declining health— he found that

> Only what word
> Wisest my heart breeds dark heaven's baffling ban
> Bars or hell's spell thwarts.

Whatever he begins he is unable to bring to an end: either he must needs hoard the word 'unheard' by others, or if he does manage to make it heard it only passes 'unheeded'. So he feels himself 'Time's eunuch', forever fruitless, and unable to 'breed one work that wakes'.

Thus it is that, in spite of himself, and 'frantic to avoid' what seems an inevitable fate, he enters into the period known to mystics as the 'dark night of the senses'. Nor is it the first time he has entered into this night. Already he has described a similar experience in *The Wreck of the Deutschland*; which begins from 'The swoon of a heart that the sweep and the hurl of thee trod / Hard down with a horror of height'. He now recurs to this experience of 'now done darkness', when he felt himself in his dark ecstasy to be (like Jacob with the Angel) wrestling even with God. Only now the wrestling is more lingering, longer drawn out; and God is no longer present to him, even in disguise as the 'hound of heaven', but absent and strangely silent. His lament he utters in 'cries countless'; but his cries are 'like dead letters sent / To dearest him that lives alas! away.'

There is deep inspiration in these 'dark' sonnets, even—paradoxically—in their complaints of 'lagging lines' that lack 'The roll, the rise, the carol, the creation' of true poetry. But the inspiration is of a different kind from that of the 'bright' sonnets: it is that of a 'winter world' as contrasted with the richness and variety of the springtime of nature around him. No longer, as in the 'bright' sonnets, does he draw upon the imagery of the outside world, as he had described it so minutely and delicately in his English Journal. Now instead he looks within his mind; and there he sees strange 'sights' and bewildering 'ways'—mountains of the mind, compared with which those in Wales and the Pennines are mere molehills. He can no longer find delight in the variety of nature in daytime, but can only scrutinize his inner thoughts that seem to grind one against another. He can no longer take pleasure in the selfhood or 'thisness' of things, but can only observe his 'self-yeast of spirit' souring the 'dull dough' of his being, and 'live', as it were enclosed by endless mirrors of selves, 'this tormented mind / With this tormented mind tormenting yet'.

There is something abstract about the expression of these poems, though in their meaning they are intense and immediate enough. There is little or nothing in them that lends itself to visual illustration, save by way of a phantasmal succession of unrelated images. Thus we read: 'My cries heave, herds-long; huddle in a main, a chief- / woe, world-sorrow'—where from the sound of 'cries' the poet moves to the image of 'herds' of cattle driven along a country road, then to that of a 'main' or sea into which pour the rivers of his woe and which is compared to a 'world', before going on to the further image of an 'age-old anvil'. These images coexist, not in the sunlit world of nature, but in a nightmare of the poet's own—one is tempted to say distraught—imagination. It should, however, be added that these 'dark' sonnets are for the most part concentrated, or 'huddle in a main', in one year and one portion of that year, the late spring and early summer of 1885. After that there are indeed intermittent spells of darkness, but never again anything so intense.

The long sonnet that introduces these 'dark' sonnets in most editions of Hopkins was, however, composed in the following year—as an author commonly writes his preface after the main chapters of his book. In it the poet makes a significant return to the imagery of nature to describe the experience he has just been through. Following the customary metaphor in mystical writings, he compares his experience to the approach of night, with more than an echo of the stanza in Shakespeare's Sonnet 73:

In me thou see'st the twilight of such day
As after sunset fadeth in the west;
Which by and by black night doth take away,
Death's second self, that seals up all in rest.

The title of his sonnet, however, he takes not from evening or night, but from 'Sibyl's leaves'—that is, the leaves of paper on which the Sibyl (as described by Virgil in *Aeneid* VI) would write down her oracles or prophecies, only to have them scattered by the wind. For him the leaves are the elements of 'earth's dapple', set 'astray or aswarm' by the gathering darkness; and putting them together, he finds they spell out a Sibylline oracle, reminiscent of the funereal hymn *Dies Irae: 'Dies irae, dies illa, solvet saeclum in favilla, teste David cum Sibylla'*—Day of wrath (or divine judgment), that day shall dissolve this world in ashes, as David and the Sibyl foretold (referring to the Messianic age).

The poet begins his poem with a presentation of 'evening' in an impressive series of epithets, testifying to the seriousness and solemnity of the time. The first few have ominously open vowels, symbolic in the very openness of their sound of the openness of their sense. There are similar effects in *The Wreck of the Deutschland*: 'And after it almost unmade', and 'The infinite air is unkind'. As for the individual epithets, 'earnest' has the meaning of tense or strained seriousness, and aptly anticipates the main verb, 'strains'. It is also used of the sky by Hopkins in his Journal for 1871: 'The higher, zenith sky earnest and frowning.' 'Earthless' has an implication of remote aloofness, as of the gods of Epicurus and Lucretius. Its significance is indicated in another passage from the Journal for 1870: 'This busy working of nature wholly independent of the earth and seeming to go on in a strain of time not reckoned by our reckoning of days and years.' The same thought interestingly recurs in a passage of T. S. Eliot's *Dry Salvages*. 'Equal' refers to the levelling of the variety of nature, brought on by the evening; and metaphorically to the impartiality of divine justice, rendered to each man after death according to his works. 'Vaulty' alludes to the round vault of heaven, which is revealed in the night-time as 'still higher', and recalls 'the dark side of the bay of thy blessing' in *The Wreck of the Deutschland* which serves to 'vault' the victims amid their disaster. 'Voluminous' has the general feeling of immensity and depth of dimension, combined with the possible image of volumes or scrolls as oracles of the future—as well as the further suggestion of 'luminous' in the stars. Lastly, after a telling pause, comes 'stupendous', by which the poet stresses his sense of awe and terror at the implications of the scene.

In their totality these epithets of evening insist on one direction: namely, the approach of night. So night, in turn, is characterized by a further series of epithets. In the first place, it is the night of time—both as belonging to time (in a possessive sense) and as including time (in an objective sense). For time, too, has to come to an end with the end of time. Secondly, it is 'vast', with a combined sense of immensity and devastation, and an echo from *Hamlet* i.2: 'In the dead vast and middle of the night'. Thirdly, it is all-inclusive, as 'womb-of-all', the mother from whose capacious womb all things come forth; as 'home-of-all', the dwelling from which all things come in the morning and to which they return in the evening; as 'hearse-of-all', the grave or tomb in which all things are finally buried. Elsewhere, in *The Wreck of the Deutschland*, the poet uses the same metaphor, 'Warm-laid grave of a womb-life grey'; and in both cases he seems to be echoing Friar Laurence's remark in *Romeo and Juliet*: 'The earth that's nature's mother is her tomb.'

He goes on to describe a particular scene after sunset, before 'the last lights off the black West' have all gone. Amid the gathering dusk there still lingers a glow of 'yellow hornlight' on the western horizon. He speaks of it as 'fond', in that the evening seems to cling to it as a fond father, unwilling to let it go; yet as 'wound to the west', in that the source of the light has already wound or wended its way below the western horizon. As for 'hornlight', it may be variously identified as the 'horny rays' of the sun, which the poet mentions on several occasions in his Journal as coming from behind a cloud; or (preferably) as the effect of pale yellow light gleaming through the horny thinness of a horn-lantern. This is implied in another passage of the Journal for 1873: 'Westward lamping with tipsy bufflight, the colour of yellow roses.' It is hardly the light of the horned moon, as has been suggested.

In contrast to the 'yellow hornlight' slowly disappearing from the horizon, there is another kind of light appearing 'hung to the height' which is characterized as 'wild hollow hoarlight'. Elsewhere the poet speaks of it as 'hoary-glow height'—a cold white light, as of hoar frost, high up in the heavens. There is something exceedingly ancient about this light, as it appears in the evening sky, reminding men of an earlier and greater creation. It is also 'wild' and 'hollow', including within itself the vast womb of chaos, yet remaining empty in its unlimited concavity. Finally, the description of 'hoarlight' is effectively rounded off with the epithet 'waste', standing as it does in monosyllabic solitude at the beginning of the next line and in a resoundingly predicative position. It serves to emphasize that all is but a vast and empty desert, whose silences terrified the speculative soul of Pascal. To interpret it as a verb, whether intransitive or transitive (with 'us' as object), immeasurably weakens its force.

Gradually, as the 'hoarlight' itself fades away, there appear from out of the waste tract of sky the 'earliest stars' of the evening. Not only are they 'earliest stars' in point of time, but also 'earlstars' in point of dignity and precedence. They are the 'principalities and powers' of which Saint Paul speaks in his letter to the Ephesians (vi); they are the 'rulers of the world of this darkness'. As such, they 'overbend us', in the sense of overseeing all our actions and overawing our minds and imaginations in 'this bent world'. All together they appear as 'fíre-féaturing heaven', in an inscape that inspires many of the poems and much of the Journal of Hopkins. He is filled with enthusiasm as he looks up at the stars on a clear night, and imagines them as 'fire-folk sitting in the air'. He listens to them as 'belled fire', and even feels them as 'the moth-soft Milky Way', naming them 'what by your measure is the heaven of desire'. But here he does not dwell on their sight with enthusiasm: other in measure is his mind's burden.

For while the stars have been coming out one by one, the earth has been disappearing into darkness—at least, in all her variety of form and colour. It is as if she has 'unbound', or unmade, her very being, consisting as this does (on analogy with the human body) of bones and veins bound together, and fastened with flesh. The dapple of her 'pied beauty', with its 'landscape plotted and pieced', is now 'at an end'; and the various elements that composed it are either 'astray or aswarm', scattered like leaves to the winds, or merging into one another without distinction, 'all throughther, in throngs'. Above all, the prized self-hood of things, that which in the light of day 'flashes off frame and face', is now dissolved and destroyed—'steeped and pashed'—in the darkness of night. All things are now 'dismembered', torn as it were limb from limb, and 'disremembered', buried in formless oblivion.

So from the darkness of the world around him the poet turns to reflect on himself and the oracular significance of all he has seen. He speaks, in a characteristic yet Biblical manner, to his own heart, which is (as he declares in *The Wreck of the Deutschland*) at once 'unteachably after evil' and yet 'uttering truth'. In its latter capacity it now rounds upon him in a whisper (to combine two meanings of 'rounds' in a single expression) and puts the situation frankly before him. All, it shows him, is but a parable of what is to happen to himself, and to all mankind. It is not only an evening of nature, but the evening of human life that is 'over us'; and the approach of night is 'our night', that is to say, 'death and the dark'. For him and for all mankind, all is to be 'in an unfathomable, . . . in an enormous dark / Drowned'; and he is overwhelmed by the thought, as he will be by the reality when it comes.

Meanwhile, he notices the 'beak-leaved boughs' silhouetted in 'dragon-ish' shapes against the pale light that lingers in the west—just as Mark Antony shortly before his death in *Antony and Cleopatra* speaks of 'a cloud that's dragonish' as part of 'black vesper's pageants' that soon dislimn. They produce what he calls in his Journal an effect of 'damasking in the sky', like the intricate patterns inlaid on the smooth blades of damascened swords. They symbolize the nightmare fears of death that come crowd-ing into his imagination. For the moment there is still some 'bleak light'; but soon all will be black, 'ever so black'. Then 'Manshape, that shone / Sheer off, disseveral, a star, death blots black out'. Yet in this very dark-ness the poet sees a light: he recognizes it as 'Oúr tale, O oúr oracle!'

In the light of this discovery he cannot lament his fate with 'pity and indignation', as he affects to do in the companion piece, *That Nature is a Heraclitean Fire*. Instead, he reveals an unexpected spirit of resignation, kissing the divine rod as in *Carrion Comfort*, and following the advice of *The Golden Echo*: 'Resign them, sign them, seal them, send them . . . Give beauty back, beauty, beauty, beauty, back to God, beauty's self and beauty's giver.' 'Let life', he exclaims, now that it has 'waned' or declined into its evening of 'the sere, the yellow leaf', 'lét life wind / Off hér once skéined stained véined varíety upon, áll on twó spools.' The rich variety of form and colour in every vein of 'earth's sweet being' he compares to woollen threads of diverse colours wound severally in many skeins. But now is the time, he declares, for the threads to be unwound and rewound on two spools, without regarding their precise hue, but only dividing them according to their general shade. Another comparison he uses is that of Christ himself, in his parable of the judgment (*Matt.* xxv). Things in their varied selfhood are seen as sheep roaming over the meadows for pasture during the day. But now is the time for them to be gathered together, parted, penned and packed into two folds: one black and the other white, or (as in Christ's parable) one of sheep and the other of goats.

In short, the approach of night is seen by the poet as an oracle, not just of death, but of the judgment that follows on death. There before the seat of the heavenly Judge, as Claudius fully realized in the prayer scene in *Hamlet*, 'the action lies in his true nature': things are seen in their fundamental colours of 'black, white', and actions are seen in their ultimate values of 'right, wrong'. Apart from these two values, after all, nothing really matters in the long run. They are the only two things we should reckon on, mind about; since they are the only things that count in the day of judgment. Yet 'dear and dogged man', as he is described in *Ribblesdale*, remains 'so tied to his turn, / To thriftless reave both our rich round world bare / And none reck of world after'. So the poet ends his sonnet with a word of caution, while we still enjoy the evening of life, to be 'wáre of a wórld where bút these twó tell'—that is, to take thought for the life after death, where all depends on our deeds in this world, whether right or wrong.

Finally, he adds a further grim warning of the punishment that is to overtake wrong deeds, a 'rack' far worse than that of 'this tough world', 'Where, selfwrung, selfstrung, sheathe- and shelterless, thóughts agaínst thoughts ín groans grínd'. This is a rack on which the selfish self is left to itself with nothing to distract or disguise its foul selfishness from itself. For hell, as Hopkins realizes in common with Christian tradition, is not so much what God inflicts on the lost soul as what the lost soul inflicts on itself, having turned away from God. 'Their scourge', as he says in another sonnet, is merely to be 'their sweating selves'. Yet in his own experience of the dark night of the senses, he feels as if he has come very close to their condition—even while clinging to God in the depths of his being. It is precisely from out of these depths that he voices his earnest warning concerning man's earthless destiny; and so he concludes this introduction to his 'dark' sonnets, having completed what he calls (in a letter to Bridges) 'the longest sonnet ever made and no doubt the longest making'.

12
Favoured Make and Mind

A Brother and Sister
O I admire and sorrow! The heart's eye grieves
Discovering you, dark tramplers, tyrant years.
A juice rides rich through bluebells, in vine leaves,
And beauty's dearest veriest vein is tears.

Happy the father, mother of these! Too fast:
Not that, but thus far, all with frailty, blest
In one fair fall; but, for time's aftercast,
Creatures all heft, hope, hazard, interest.

And are they thus? The fine, the fingering beams
Their young delightful hour do feature down
That fleeted else like day-dissolvèd dreams
Or ringlet-race on burling Barrow brown.

She leans on him with such contentment fond
As well the sister sits, would well the wife;
His looks, the soul's own letters, see beyond,
Gaze on, and fall directly forth on life.

But ah, bright forelock, cluster that you are
Of favoured make and mind and health and youth,
Where lies your landmark, seamark, or soul's star?
There's none but truth can stead you. Christ is truth.

There's none but good can bé good, both for you
And what sways with you, maybe this sweet maid;
None good but God—a warning wavèd to
One once that was found wanting when Good weighed.

Man lives that list, that leaning in the will
No wisdom can forecast by gauge or guess,
The selfless self of self, most strange, most still,
Fast furled and all foredrawn to No or Yes.

Your feast of; that most in you earnest eye
May but call on your banes to more carouse.
Worst will the best. What worm was here, we cry,
To have havoc-pocked so, see, the hung-heavenward boughs?

Enough: corruption was the world's first woe.
What need I strain my heart beyond my ken?
O but I bear my burning witness though
Against the wild and wanton work of men.

.   .   .   .

On the Portrait of Two Beautiful Young People

In his poetic appreciation of 'mortal beauty', Hopkins includes no less
'the human form divine' than the inscapes of the natural world around
him. He is particularly attracted to the 'innocent mind and Mayday in
girl and boy', which he celebrates in poem after poem; though he turns
his thoughts rather to male than to female beauty, characterizing it in
The Bugler's First Communion as 'bloom of a chastity in mansex fine'. He
takes delight in 'beauty's bearing' as discerned in 'the handsome heart' of
a child, not so much in itself as in its being 'bathed in high hallowing
grace'. He takes similar delight in the loveliness of love between boys
who are brothers, where the life of one is 'all laced', even 'lóve-laced', in
that of the other.

Yet his appreciation of beauty is not unqualified. It is almost invariably
mingled with anxiety, both for himself as the admiring subject and for
the object of his admiration. On the one hand, as he warns himself as
well as the reader in his sonnet *To what serves Mortal Beauty?*, such beauty
is 'dangerous; does set dancing blood'. It appeals to that source of
corruption in man which is traditionally termed 'concupiscence', or
excessive desire to possess the object for oneself. This is why he urgently
advises, in the conclusion of the sonnet:

> Merely meet it; own,
> Home at heart, heaven's sweet gift; | then leave, let that alone.

For the corruption is, fundamentally, an inclination to make an idol of what is merely mortal, and so to deprive God of the glory that belongs to him alone. It is therefore imperative, while recognizing the 'mortal beauty' in man, to desire in and above all 'God's better beauty, grace'.

On the other hand, for the object of his admiration, 'those lovely lads', the poet feels an even more anxious fear, as a father for his growing children. He is afraid their innocence may all too soon 'cloy', 'cloud' and 'sour with sinning', owing to a strain of wildness and wantonness deep in the nature of 'dear and dogged man'. He feels as Teryth felt for his daughter Winefred, how

> The deeper grows her dearness
> And more and more times laces ¹ round and round my heart,
> The more some monstrous hand ¹ gropes with clammy fingers there,
> Tampering with those sweet bines

Even from a distance he observes men going by him 'whom either beauty bright / In mould or mind or what not else makes rare'; and he grieves over the thought that 'Death or distance soon consumes them'.

For this reason he is all the more insistent on the importance of sacrifice, no less for himself than for others, as the only means of ensuring the permanence of beauty that seems so fleeting. Just as he tells himself to 'leave, let that alone', even so his advice to others in whom he finds 'all this beauty blooming' is to 'give God while worth consuming', to 'take as for tool, not toy meant' and to 'hold at Christ's employment'. Here is, above all, the meaning of *The Golden Echo*, which contains the contrast, so deeply imprinted in all Hopkins's poetry, between

> The flower of beauty, fleece of beauty, too too apt to, ah! to fleet,
> Never fleets móre, fastened with the tenderest truth
> To its own best being and its loveliness of youth:

and the need to 'Give beauty back, beauty, beauty, beauty, back to God', 'beauty's self and beauty's giver'. It is he alone who can preserve beauty from mortal corruption, keeping it as he does with 'fonder a care' than ourselves. It is for us to follow 'Yonder', beyond 'death and the dark', with the trusting spirit of a child.

All this wealth of meaning is somehow compressed within the opening words of Hopkins's poem *On the Portrait of Two Beautiful Young People: A Brother and Sister*. The portrait he saw while visiting a house at Monasterevan (originally, the monastery of St Eiminhe), a town in county Kildare situated to the south-west of Dublin. In it a young boy and girl are depicted looking out from a double wreath of bluebells and vine-leaves in the somewhat sentimental style of early Victorianism. But the poet overlooks the pretty-pretty sentimentality of the style, and attends only to the winsome features of the children. 'O I admire', he exclaims, 'and sorrow'. He admires what he sees in the actuality of the picture; but he sorrows at the thought of what lies in store for the children as 'shades of the prison-house close round' them in later years.

So in the opening stanza of the poem he goes on to develop this feeling of sorrow, rather than that of admiration. The physical eye may see and admire the present beauty of the children; but 'the heart's eye'—what Wordsworth calls 'that inward eye'—grieves at what it discovers in the future, in the trampling, unrelenting course of the 'tyrant years'. In this mention of 'the heart's eye' there is an implication, in sound and sense, of 'Natural heart's ivy, Patience', which—as the poet remarks in one of his 'dark' sonnets—'masks / Our ruins of wrecked past purpose'; and of what he calls in *The Wreck of the Deutschland* 'that asking for ease / Of the sodden-with-its-sorrowing heart'. Also in the gem-like epithet, 'dark tramplers', is contained a further implication from *God's Grandeur* of generations that 'have trod, have trod, have trod'.

For the time being, as he notes in the flowery wreaths framing the children's faces, there is 'a juice' that 'rides rich through bluebells, in vine leaves'—or, as he identifies it in *Spring*, 'A strain of the earth's sweet being in the beginning'. But, he adds, with a melancholy echo of Virgil's famous *Sunt lacrimae rerum*, 'beauty's dearest veriest vein is tears'. The contemplation of beauty cannot but draw tears from the eyes; and yet it is somehow through 'the mist of tears' that we retrieve the freshness of beauty in a new life.

Considering the present beauty of the children, the poet cannot forbear to bless their parents: 'Happy the father, mother of these!'—as it were echoing the words of the woman in the Gospel who uttered a similar blessing on Christ: 'Blessed is the womb that bore you!' But he immediately checks himself with 'Too fast!'—as it were recalling the reminder of Sophocles in the chorus of *Oedipus Tyrannus*: 'Call no man happy!' It is dangerous for a man to praise other mortals, lest he only draw down the jealousy of the gods on their momentary happiness and thus bring it to an untimely end.

Again, however, he checks himself, qualifying 'Too fast' with 'Not that, but', an inverted form of 'Not but what'. Up till now, he admits, the parents—for all their human frailty, and subject as they are to corruption and misfortune—have indeed been blest in the 'day's dear chance' which brought them such children (so, presumably, twins) 'in one fair fall'. This last phrase recalls the opening line of *Henry Purcell*: 'Have fair fallen, O fair, fair have fallen'. Only there it is an optative reference to the moment of death and wished-for rebirth: here it is rather to the moment of birth in the indicative past. As such it also recalls the 'Fresh-firecoal chestnut-falls' of *Pied Beauty* and the 'wet-fresh windfalls of war's storm' of *To what serves Mortal Beauty?* But then the poet adds a further qualification, to recover his original meaning in 'Too fast', considering not 'thus far', but 'for time's aftercast'—looking, like Shelley, not only 'before' but also 'after', and pining 'for what is not'.

From this point of view, which has engendered his sorrow and anxiety, these 'two beautiful young people' are 'creatures all' imbued with 'heft, hope, hazard, interest'. Each of these words bears its load of implication. 'Heft', besides its echo of 'tender-hefted nature' from *King Lear*, contains the perfect form of 'heaving' as with sighs of sorrow or aspirations for future joy. 'Hope' expresses the optimistic side of 'heft', in contrast to despair which supervenes in the frustrated course of time. 'Hazard' envisages the element of chance and fortune that fills the span of human life and bids us wear 'brows of such care, care and deep concern'. 'Interest' recalls the moving light in *The Lantern out of Doors* which so interested the poet's eyes and led him to wonder 'where from and bound . . . where'. He would like to 'wind' his 'eye after' the light, but resigns himself to the thought that he cannot 'be in at the end'. All he can do is to commit the man to 'Christ's interest', who follows him as his 'first, fást, last friénd'.

His anxious expectation for the future is, however, once again checked by the question: 'And are they thus?'—as it were echoing Sir Thomas Wyatt's question: 'And wilt thou leave me thus?' in an opposite sense. For as Keats had earlier noted in his *Ode on a Grecian Urn*, there is already something immortal in the beauty recorded in this portrait. The skilful fingers of the artist have succeeded in imprisoning the delicate 'beams' of light in his lines and colours, and in 'featuring'—or capturing forever the features of—'their young delightful hour'. Without his intervention that hour would have disappeared as swiftly as a dream dissolves with the approach of day, or as the eddies or ringlets pass away on the surface of the rich brown current of the river Barrow (which flows southward past Monasterevan to Waterford harbour). The strong, rounded movement of the river is characterized as 'burling', a favourite inscape word of the poet which he uses elsewhere with a similar meaning: in *the Wreck of the Deutschland*, 'the burl of the fountains of air', and 'wind's burly and beat of endragonèd seas'; and in the Journal, 'the burly water-backs', and 'the burling and roundness of the world'.

So for the moment he fixes his attention on the present, and studies the portrait as a work of art. He admires the way the sister leans on her brother 'with such contentment fond'. He reflects how this same love would be no less fitting in a wife for her husband, with a possible reminiscence of Milton's description of the ideal love of Adam and Eve in *Paradise Lost* Book IV. Then, turning from the sister to the brother, he notes that, instead of looking reciprocally back on her, he directs his gaze outward on the world and on life. For the man, as Saint Paul says in *Ephesians*, is the head of the woman: she looks to him, and he looks to the outer world and to God. Hence in the brother's looks the poet recognizes 'the soul's own letters', written not to another being like himself, but to him who is 'beyond', even if he does not yet fully know his divine identity. The same image appears, in a different context, in one of the 'dark' sonnets, where his 'cries countless' are compared to 'dead letters sent / To dearest him that lives alas! away'.

Once again the poet finds he cannot long remain on the thought of the present, even of the eternal present of art. He is ever being carried onwards by his human imagination and his thoughts and fears for the future. The very fairness of the forehead and 'bright forelock' of the children, and the very framing of their 'favoured make and mind and health and youth' in wreaths of leaves and flowers, only elicit a deep sigh: 'But ah!' They also prompt him to put the all-important question, on which their future depends: 'Where lies your landmark, seamark, or soul's star?' For without truth to keep them steady, it will not be long before their 'mark on mind' is gone, when death comes and blots them 'black out'. As a priest, he has no doubt where that truth is to be found. What Wordsworth vaguely calls 'our life's star', Hopkins identifies more personally and precisely as Christ, who said of himself: 'I am the way, the truth, and the life.'

He therefore goes on to recall a favourite passage from the gospels, the story of the rich young man. Coming to Jesus, the young man asked: 'Good Master, what shall I do to receive life everlasting?' But Jesus reproved him: 'Why do you call me good? None is good but one, that is God.' Then, as Saint Mark records, Jesus 'looking on him, loved him'; and he went on to say: 'One thing is wanting to you: go, sell whatever you have and give it to the poor, and you shall have treasure in heaven; then come, follow me.' At this, the young man turned away sadly, for he could not bring himself to give up his possessions. With this story in his mind, the poet emphasizes that only Christ, who is God, can be good, both for the boy himself and for 'this sweet maid' who maybe 'sways with' him in his affection. This warning Christ made to the rich young man, but found him wanting when his 'poising palms were weighing the worth' in the balance. Let them learn from his lesson.

Thus the poet draws his characteristic conclusion about Man, with his Scotist preference of will over intellect. What is deepest, most essential in human life, he insists, is 'that list, that leaning in the will', which is beyond the power of human wisdom to 'forecast by gauge or guess'. There is a bias or bent in the deepest heart of man, in the inmost 'self of self', where paradoxically man is most 'selfless', as most ready to respond to the call of another. This response, which is given when 'the heart, being hard at bay, is out with it', is either 'No or Yes', either the worst or the best word, either rejection or acceptance of the divine invitation. This readiness of the heart is expressed in terms of a nautical metaphor, of a ship with her sails all trim, 'fast furled and all foredrawn'. So it is not surprising to find the same repeated with variations in the two poems of shipwreck: not only (as we have seen) in *The Wreck of the Deutschland*, but also in *The Loss of the Eurydice*, where the poet admires how 'At downright "No or Yes?" ' even one who is 'in mankind's medley a duty-swerver' often 'doffs all, drives full for righteousness'.

In the order of 'No or Yes' there is an implicit emphasis on the final 'Yes', showing the poet's hope that this is what the two young people will eventually choose. At the same time, he cannot shake off his fear that after all one of them may say 'No'; and in the next stanza he gives expression to his fear. He speaks of their 'feast of' plenty (understood in the abrupt pause of an ellipsis), as the object of 'their young delightful hour', and of their 'earnest eye' (literally, 'that most in you earnest eye'), as the subject of this delight; but he is afraid that both may but serve to call down the jealous fates (Anglo-Saxon 'banes') to rejoice all the more in their undoing, like the Fury in the 'dark' sonnet *No worst*. Somehow in this fallen world it is 'the best' which invites the 'worst' to do his worst upon—*corruptio optimi pessima*. It is precisely 'the hung-heavenward boughs', which 'so sigh deep poetry' to the mind of the poet, that become most 'havoc-pocked' and consumed by worms of corruption— as a fair, soft-faced infant all too often grows into an adolescent afflicted by skin disease.

But now the poet breaks off—as at the end of his long sonnet *That Nature is a Heraclitean Fire*—with 'Enough'. 'Corruption', he remarks, may have been 'the world's first woe', through the original sin of Adam; but that is no reason why it should end all things, too. 'Why', he asks himself, 'need I strain my heart beyond my ken?' In a similar vein he exhorts himself in one of his 'dark' sonnets, 'My own heart let me more have pity on', and 'Call off thoughts awhile'. Why strain his eyes, peering into an uncertain future, which is all the more uncertain as it concerns not himself, but these two others. It should be sufficient for him to commit them to the fond care of Christ.

All the same, he justifies his task and his intention in this unfinished poem, to bear 'burning witness' in his loving zeal 'Against the wild and wanton work of men'. What he eagerly wants is for 'Jessy or Jack there', the sister or the brother, or rather both together, 'God to aggrandise, God to glorify'. What, on the other hand, he sadly deprecates is the way man grows with the passing of the 'tyrant years', 'to his own self bent so bound, so tied to his turn', and comes to reck nothing 'of world after'.

This 'witness', however, he leaves unfinished, perhaps because it is—paradoxically enough—insufficiently qualified. 'The wild and wanton work of men' is an ending as conclusive in sound as one might wish for in a poem. Yet the whole is included among the unfinished poems of Hopkins, ending not with 'men', but with an inconclusive line of dots. For there is something inconclusive about the sense: there is at least the suggestion of a need for self-rebuke to follow, as in *The Candle Indoors*, where the poet qualifies his 'burning witness' by rounding on himself with the indignant 'Come you indoors, come home'. Or he may have felt that with so many qualifications in his poem he had left himself without the means of pulling it together in any convincing unity. Or possibly he may have preferred to leave his poem in its unfinished state, the better to symbolize the unfinished lives of the two children and his own unfinished consciousness concerning them. Who can tell? Perhaps too, for the same reason, it may be fitting to leave this chapter in a similarly unfinished state. . . .

13
This Dry Dean

O now while skies are blue, | now while seas are salt,
While rushy rains shall fall | or brooks shall fleet from fountains,
While sick men shall cast sighs, | of sweet health all despairing,
While blind men's eyes shall thírst after | daylight, draughts of daylight,
Or deaf ears shall desire that | lípmusic that's lóst upon them,
While cripples are, while lepers, | dancers in dismal limb-dance,
Fallers in dreadful frothpits, | waterfearers wild,
Stone, palsy, cancer, cough, | lung-wasting, womb-not-bearing,
Rupture, running sores, | what more? in brief, in burden,
As long as men are mortal | and God merciful,
So long to this sweet spot, | this leafy lean-over,
This Dry Dean, nów no longer dry | nor dumb, but moist and musical
With the uproll and the downcarol | of day and night delivering
Water, which keeps thy name, | (for not in róck written,
But in pale water, fráil water, | wild rash and reeling water,
That will not wear a print, | that will not stain a pen,
Thy venerable record, | virgin, is recorded).
Here to this holy well | shall pilgrimages be,
And not from purple Wales only | nor from elmy England,
But from beyond seas, Erin, | France and Flanders, everywhere,
Pilgrims, still pilgrims, móre | pilgrims, still more poor pilgrims.

    .   .   .   .

What sights shall be when some | that swung, wretches, on crutches
Their crutches shall cast from them, | on heels of air departing,
Or they go rich as roseleaves | hence that loathsome cáme hither!
Not now to náme even
Those dearer, more divine | boons whose haven the heart is.

    .   .   .   .

As sure as what is most sure, | sure as that spring primroses

Shall new-dapple next year, | sure as to-morrow morning,
Amongst come-back again things, | thíngs with a revival, things with a
   recovery,
Thy name . . .

    .   .   .   .

St Winefred's Well: Part C

With his emphasis on man's place at the centre of the natural world, and
his stress on the dynamism of divine energy within both man and the
natural world—'Since, tho' he is under the world's splendour and wonder, /
His mystery must be instressed, stressed'—there is inevitably a feeling of
high drama in Hopkins's poems. As a follower of Duns Scotus, as well as
of Saint Ignatius Loyola, he is not content with a merely speculative,
intellectual approach to the universe; but everywhere he discerns a
dynamic presence of will, derived from the first creative *fiat* of God and
requiring in return an energetic response from man. Moreover, as an
admirer of Shakespeare, as well as of Milton and Wordsworth, he cannot
but feel in his poetic response to nature and nature's God a strong urge to
dramatize this response out of the rich resources provided for him in
Shakespeare's plays. In one of his letters he admits, it is true, that the
example of Shakespeare 'has done ever so much harm by his very
genius'; and he explains his meaning, remarking that 'poets reproduce
the diction which in him was modern and in them is obsolete'. Yet as a
Romantic poet himself, he is lured, almost in spite of himself, to
attempt a task which so many Romantic poets have likewise attempted—
to their own undoing. Thus it is that among his poems we find one
drama, *St Winefred's Well*; but it is, significantly, one of his unfinished
poems.

    What Hopkins admires in Shakespeare is naturally his poetic
language—even if much of it seems to him obsolete (though it must have
sounded as 'obsolete' in Elizabethan as in Victorian ears). What he also
admires is his power in portraying the inner character and motives of
individual men. In other words, what he admires is more or less what
Milton and the subsequent Romantic poets admired in Shakespeare: not
so much his dramatic technique or development of plot, as his rich and
complex analysis of human character, not so much in action as in
dialogue, and most of all in soliloquy. In fact, one might say that
Hopkins approached Shakespeare not only through the grand soliloquies
of a Hamlet, a Macbeth and an Othello, but also as they came to him
filtered through the great speeches of Satan in *Paradise Lost*. His approach

may still be described as dramatic, but with a preference for dramatic poetry rather than for dramatic performance.

Here is perhaps the fundamental reason why, when he came to compose his first and only drama, it remained in a fragmentary form. In a letter to Bridges he spurned the suggestion that he had deliberately aimed at writing 'fragments of a dramatic poem' in much the same spirit as Victorian enthusiasts for Gothic might have medieval 'ruins' constructed in their grounds. What he had written, he maintained, he had written as mere drafts of a drama which he hoped—with his friend's encouragement—to complete in due time; and if he had failed to complete it, this was due not to any indulgence in archaism, but to unfavourable circumstances that made him unable 'to go on with *Winefred* or anything else'. All the same, it is not without significance that—however unfavourable may have been the circumstances of its composition—the fragments of *St Winefred's Well* which he submitted to his friend's inspection in 1885 were for the most part soliloquies spoken by the three main characters of the drama. The first is spoken by Teryth, Winefred's father; the second, by Caradoc, her lover and murderer; and the third by Lord Beuno, her uncle and restorer to life. They are presented by the poet as fragments; but in fact they have a certain unity and ideal inter-connection, forming respectively the beginning, middle and end of a dramatic vision of the saint and of the place associated with her name—the shrine of Holywell in the county of Flintshire, only eight or nine miles from St Beuno's College.

The first of these fragments begins, it is true, with a dialogue between Teryth and his daughter; but the dialogue is brief and serves merely to introduce the girl as it were in a fleeting glimpse, possibly with the consideration that 'a glance master more may than gaze, gaze out of countenance'. From this brief exchange, which seems rather awkward in naturalistic terms, we gather the poet's intention to present Winefred as another Desdemona ('A maiden never bold; / Of spirit so still and quiet, that her motion / Blush'd at herself') or Cordelia (whose 'voice was ever soft', / Gentle and low, an excellent thing in woman'). There is something charming in her fewness of words, her modest demeanour, her delight at the news of her uncle's approach, her readiness to comply with her father's wishes. That is all; but it is enough to give point to the soliloquies that follow. She is hardly a character in the play, but a spirit behind all the characters.

Now Teryth, left to himself, reflects in a characteristically Hopkinsian manner on the beauty of his daughter and his own parental affection for her, but also on the fear which her beauty and his affection somehow inspires in him. For what he loves so dearly may become morally corrupted in itself, or physically removed from him; and either case is fraught with tragedy. He compares the gradual growth of his affection to tendrils of woodbine or honeysuckle growing 'round and round my heart'. But he feels 'some monstrous hand' that 'with clammy fingers' is groping and tampering with the 'sweet bines'. He sweats for fear, and forebodes—already from the beginning—the end of her 'funeral'. Yet he realizes that it is not so much a funeral as 'some pageant', a religious procession of pilgrim's to a martyr's shrine. This thought, as with Lear, brings 'all the mother' to his eyes; and, in spite of himself, he breaks out—like the poet himself in *The Wreck of the Deutschland*—in tears, 'such a melting, a madrigal start'.

This opening celebration of the ideal relationship between father and daughter, however, occupies less space in the dramatic poem, and presumably less interest in the poet's mind, than the long soliloquy which follows—after a gap—when Caradoc enters with his bloody sword after the murder. The Shakespearian influence is here apparent throughout—particularly from Othello's soliloquy before his murder of Desdemona; though it is strangely overlaid by the Miltonic influence—from Satan's defiant speeches in the first book of *Paradise Lost*. On the one hand, Caradoc is presented lamenting over the maiden he has just murdered, and mouthing imitations of Othello's speech. On the other hand, he is made to justify his deed with a Satanic hypocrisy, in words that are oddly inconsistent with his previous utterances—no doubt, to dramatize the conflict that has arisen within him as a result of having hacked his being 'in half with hér neck'. Like Macbeth, he is aware of having given the eternal jewel of his soul 'to the common enemy of man'; but unlike any Shakespearian hero, and only like Milton's Satan, he defends his action in 'a wide world of defiance', as having in itself 'a sweetness, . . . a kind of joy in it, a zest, an edge, an ecstasy'. Then on the approach of 'Mankind, that mob', he closes his soliloquy and fades 'out of sight' and 'out of mind'.

Last comes the speech of Lord Beuno, who enters—according to the stage direction—'After Winefred's raising from the dead and the breaking out of the fountain'. It is delivered in the tradition of 'apotheosis' which belongs not so much to drama, as to pastoral and elegiac poetry—as in Virgil's *Eclogue VI* to Daphnis, Milton's *Lycidas* to Edward King, and Shelley's *Adonais* to John Keats. In each case a lament for an untimely death is succeeded by assurance of a continuing life in heaven. Thus it is that here, although Winefred has been raised from the dead, and her head miraculously replaced on her shoulders, her uncle's words have the effect of strangely distancing her from his hearers. She is made to appear with her continued life not so much on earth as in heaven; or rather not so much in her physical being as a human girl on earth, as in her undying memory as a saint and martyr—the object of an unending pilgrimage of devotees.

So from the beginning of his speech Beuno, as lord and bishop, looks forward in an apocalyptic vision to the end of time. He contemplates the whole intervening period between now and then, 'while skies are blue' and 'seas are salt', while rain is 'rushy' (or 'all in a rush', like 'The descending blue' of the sky in *Spring*), and brooks 'fleet' in swiftly flowing enjoyment from their fountains. He surveys the natural world, in which all things exist and act according to their kinds in sweet harmony. But he then goes on to portray man against this background as unnaturally afflicted with various kinds of diseases. There are sick men sighing in despair of 'sweet health', and blind men thirsting for 'draughts of daylight'. He associates them with his own condition of darkness, when—as he laments in the sonnet *My own heart*—he seeks a comfort he can no more get 'than blind / Eyes in their dark can (find) day or (dry mouths in their) thirst can find' water. He mentions the deaf in their longing to hear the 'lipmusic' of speech; the cripples; the lepers whose movements seem like those of skeletons in a macabre dance of death; the possessed, or epileptics, whose falling into fits and frothing at the mouth are characterized as 'dreadful frothpits'; all who are oppressed by the stone of their kidneys or bladder, by paralysis, by cancer, by coughing, by consumption of the lungs, by sterility of the womb, by hernia, by various kinds of ulcers, or by other maladies whose list is endless.

In these words Beuno passes in review the varied ills of mortal life on this earth—that life which Christ came down from heaven to share with men, so as to reveal by his miracles of healing and by his Death and Resurrection the light of divine mercy amid the darkness of human misery. His list serves to echo the Messianic prophecy of Isaiah, quoted by Christ himself to the disciples of John, that 'the blind see, the lame walk, the lepers are cleansed, the deaf hear, the dead rise again, the poor have the gospel preached to them.' Nor is it only then, in the lifetime of Christ, that this prophecy is fulfilled; but what he began in his mortal life in Palestine, he continues in his mystical life in his Church to the end of time, offering alleviation to human suffering through the miracles that continue to be worked in places consecrated by his saints. Thus not only Palestine but every land may be a holy land, a place of pilgrimage for those who believe in Christ and his saints and seek healing for themselves and their friends or relatives. Among such places is Holywell in Flintshire, where Winefred was martyred by Caradoc, and her severed head came to rest in 'this sweet spot, this leafy lean-over'. Before it was named the Dry Dean (or wooded valley), but now it is 'no longer dry', resounding as it does 'day and night' to the musical accompaniment of a spring which is ever gushing up from the earth with an 'uproll' and ever flowing down the dean with a 'downcarol'. Its water keeps the name of Winefred, both because it preserves the red mark of her blood on the stone at the bottom of the spring, and because in all its flowing it retains an inseparable association with her. Thus paradoxically her name is written in water even more enduringly than it might have been on rock. There in the pale, weak element of water, endlessly rushing down and reeling in its course, refusing to bear any imprint itself or to allow a pen to make an imprint on anything else, the virginal record of her life is forever recorded.

So in his prophetic vision Beuno foresees the streams of pilgrims that will come not only from Wales with its 'purple' mountains, or from England with its 'elmy' woods and meadows, but also 'from beyond the seas'—from Ireland, France, Belgium, and all countries in the world. Not only in the medieval 'ages of faith', but also in modern times Holywell will be known for its pilgrimages; and all who go there will be pilgrims, following one another generation upon generation in unending succession. He foresees, in particular, the many crutches adorning the shrine beside the fountain, which cripples cured in its cold waters will leave as thank-offerings to Saint Winefred. He rejoices with them, as they depart 'on heels of air', all but hurling the earth 'off under their feet' out of gratitude to Christ. He rejoices, too, with those who come hither as lepers, loathsome in appearance, and who depart with their skin restored, like that of Naaman the Syrian, to 'the velvetiness of roseleaves'. He further looks beyond the outer skin and bodily limbs to 'the handsome heart' within, where the greatest miracles are worked—with no external manifestation—as God grants his 'dearer, more divine boons', his 'high hallowing grace'.

All through this concluding prophecy Beuno makes continual reference to the name of Winefred. This it is that remains amid the changes of nature, and consecrates the natural surroundings for all time. This it is that abides as surely as primroses return to 'new-dapple' the spring of the year, as dawn reappears on 'the brown brink eastward' in the morning, as the ebbed tide rises again and recovers its domain up the shore. In short, as all the things in nature that come back come back, so surely will the name of Winefred remain alive in the memories of men.

But here Beuno breaks off, and here the poet also breaks off—as it were concluding his 'apotheosis' with an 'aposiopesis' (as in Virgil), so that 'the rest is silence'. It is as if he can no more. Not that the source of his inspiration, in contrast to Saint Winefred's well, has run dry; but that he finds words inadequate to express what he feels. So his ending on 'Thy name . . .' is all the more effective and inspiring, carrying his hearers beyond the realm of human language. Perhaps this is why he left the sentence and his whole poem incomplete. Completion he felt would only have impaired this 'unfinished symphony' which—like so many of Hopkins's poems—suggests more than it says, not only in what it says, but also in what it does not say, not only in its words of human speech, but also in its more mystical silences.

14
Wrecking and Storm

On Saturday sailed from Bremen,
  American-outward-bound,
Take settler and seamen, tell men with women,
  Two hundred souls in the round. . . .

Into the snows she sweeps,
  Hurling the haven behind,
The Deutschland, on Sunday; and so the sky keeps,
  For the infinite air is unkind. . . .

She drove in the dark to leeward,
  She struck—not a reef or a rock
But the combs of a smother of sand: night drew her
  Dead to the Kentish Knock. . . .

Hope had grown grey hairs,
  Hope had mourning on,
Trenched with tears, carved with cares,
  Hope was twelve hours gone. . . .

One stirred from the rigging to save
  The wild woman-kind below,
With a rope's end round the man, handy and brave—
  He was pitched to his death at a blow. . . .

They fought with God's cold—
  And they could not and fell to the deck
(Crushed them) or water (and drowned them) or rolled
  With the sea-romp over the wreck. . . .

from *The Wreck of the Deutschland*: Part II

If the dynamic urge in Hopkins's poetic inspiration led him eventually to undertake a dramatic poem, though unfinished, like *St Winefred's Well*, it had prompted him from the beginning to compose and complete two narrative poems, *The Wreck of the Deutschland* and *The Loss of the Eurydice*. It was, as we have seen, the narrative element—or rather, the tragedy narrated—in the former of these poems which had first unsealed Hopkins's lips after his seven years' 'elected silence' in the Society of Jesus. For there was something in his Romantic vision, as earlier in that of Wordsworth and Coleridge, which responded no less to tragedy in human life than to beauty in the world of nature, and which found its congenial utterance in terms not so much of drama as of ballad. Thus we find at the heart of the poetic structure of *The Wreck of the Deutschland*—pervasive through the poem as a whole, but more apparent in the opening stanzas of Part the Second, and in the first half of each stanza—the unmistakeable manner and rhythm of a ballad. In a subsequent letter to Bridges, Hopkins, it is true, emphasized that his poem should be treated as a Pindaric Ode and not as a narrative poem. But it is no less true that beneath the lyrical meditations with which the narrative is overlaid and wrought into an ode, there lies the essential structure of a ballad.

The heart of the poem—that in it which most immediately reflects the poet's response to the account of the tragedy, as he read it in the newspaper accounts in December, 1875—is to be found in the series of stanzas from 12–17, and in the first half of each stanza. To these one might add the introductory stanza 11, as a foreboding of what is to come, and (after a personal interruption in stanza 18) the concluding stanza 19, with the 'call of the tall nun', which is evidently for Hopkins the central point both of the story and of his poem. It was she who 'Read the unshapeable shock night' and uttered the divine word that alone gives meaning to the otherwise meaningless events in the world of men. It is, moreover, her word that prompts the poet, both in stanza 19 and in the poem as a whole, to overflow the limits of his ballad form and to impose upon them the more extended form of a Pindaric Ode.

He opens his narrative in Part the Second (the first in the order of intention) with an allegorical portrayal of Death—conceived as in a medieval Morality play, or in Chaucer's *Pardoner's Tale*, or in some Renaissance tapestry. He shows us a grim, skeletal figure beating on a drum and proclaiming the means by which Death has come (as Saint Paul says in *Romans* v) to bear sway over the world of men. Essentially, it is but a skeleton, the grinning face of Death; but outwardly, it assumes many different forms or disguises in appearing to its human victims. Now it is the 'sword' that 'gashes flesh or galls shield' amid the hurtle of 'fiercest fray' on the field of battle. Now it is the 'flange and the rail', when a man meets his death between the flashing wheels of an express locomotive and the railway line beneath. Now it is the 'flame' of a building or a forest fire, or of a 'lightning of fire hard-hurled' from the angry sky. Now it is the 'fang' of a wild animal, 'or 'beast of the waste wood', that scans 'with darksome devouring eyes the bruised bones' of its victim. Now it is the 'flood' that accompanies storms from heaven and causes rivers and seas to rise 'in high flood', ships to sink and men to drown in its 'wild waters'. It is this last-mentioned form of Death which is particularly signalized in the present poem, and emphasized by the additional background representation of storms that—like the 'naked new-born babe, / Striding the blast' in *Macbeth*—'bugle his fame'.

With this impressive introduction the poet goes on to give his simply factual, yet deeply tragic account of the shipwreck after the manner of a ballad. It is particularly remarkable how closely he keeps to the accounts of the event as given in the newspapers of the time, yet how skilfully he transforms them by the power of his words into deeply moving poetry. He begins, 'On Saturday sailed from Bremen', with what seems little more—as he remarks in a slightly different context to his friend Bridges—than 'mere Lloyd's Shipping Intelligence'. It is, in fact, just a rephrasing of the Quartermaster's report in *The Times* of 8 December: 'We left Bremen on Saturday.' He goes on, 'American-outward-bound', as a rather compressed way of stating the more customary 'outward bound for America'. He further enumerates the number of those on board, according to the report of Captain Brickenstein in *The Times* of 10 December: 'I cannot say exactly how many passengers were on board, but I believe there were about 107 emigrants with other passengers, and 99 crew'—combined with another report which is more specific: 'There were 213 souls on board the Deutschland when she struck.' He merely alters 'emigrant' to 'settler', and 'crew' to 'seamen', thereby securing an alliteration with 's' between two disyllabic words; and he uses 'tell' in his favourite sense of 'reckon' or 'enumerate' (both words used in the newspaper accounts), following on 'take', thereby securing another al-literation with 't' between two monosyllabic words. He also preserves the mention of 'souls' in the above account, not merely in the superficial sense of 'human lives', but in the deeper sense of 'immortal souls' as seen with the eye of faith from that divine point of view which is emphasized in the second half of the stanza.

From this factual opening, with its emphasis on the number of 'souls' on board, the poet goes on to describe the darkening of the weather as the ship moves into the storm. On the one hand, he still keeps close to the reports, which speak of 'the blinding snow and piercing cold'.

According to the Quartermaster, 'On Sunday morning we weighed anchor and proceeded on our voyage, a regular gale blowing at the time' (the 'regular blow' of Hopkins in the second half of this stanza). In Captain Brickenstein's report there is a precise reference to Bremerhaven, the seaport of Bremen, which Hopkins echoes in 'the haven'. On the other hand, he raises the emotional tension of his narrative by introducing a favourite pair of 'instress' words: 'sweeps' and 'hurling'. These we also find together in stanza 2: 'the sweep and the hurl of thee' (where they are used as nouns); in *The Windhover*: 'As a skate's heel sweeps smooth on a bow-bend: the hurl and gliding / Rebuffed the big wind' (where only the latter is used as a noun); and in *Ashboughs*, which, 'here, there hurled, / With talons sweep / The smouldering enormous winter welkin' (where both are verbs, but 'hurl' is used passively, and 'sweep' transitively). Here we find 'sweep' used intransitively of the forward movement of the ship, but 'hurl' transitively of what the ship does, or seems to do, to the haven (as the poet in *Hurrahing in Harvest* 'hurls earth for him off under his feet'). In contrast, however, to this dynamic movement of the ship there is an ominous feeling of suspense in the surrounding elements, 'so the sky keeps', and even more in 'the infinite air is unkind', where the alliteration with vowels suggests the openness of the elements to the influence of cosmic evil.

In the next stanza the poet continues to follow the ship's movement, only now not so much sweeping 'Into the snows' as driving 'in the dark'—no longer impulsive with dynamic force and intransitive form, but helpless and passive in force as in form, with the sense of drifting or being driven by alien forces contrary to her intention. Then he abruptly concludes the movement with 'She struck'—echoing 'the stroke dealt' in stanza 6, which (in this case) 'storms deliver'. As though to emphasize the force and nature of the impact, he does not immediately name the object, but enters as it were into the bewildered mind of those on board who are still 'in the dark' and wondering what the object can be. Evidently, from the manner of the impact, it is 'not a reef or a rock'. It can only be 'the combs of a smother of sand'—or more plainly, a shoal or sandbank. Here again the poet makes use of the reports, which state that the ship 'struck on sandbank in North sea', and 'we struck on a bank and stuck fast.' But he uses the verb 'struck' in a transitive manner, for greater effect, adding a favourite 'inscape' word, 'combs', as object for the serried edges on the surface of the sandbank, corresponding to the combs of waves such as he often describes in his Journal. He also uses the verb 'smother' as a noun, as it were arresting the effect of the sand in smothering the movement of the ship. Thus 'struck' turns out to be less sudden than at first appears; for the ship, though smothered, somehow continues to move slowly forward—till at last 'night drew her / Dead to the Kentish Knock'. Here, too, he follows the report which identifies the sandbank as the Kentish Knock, 'the outermost shoal at the mouth of the Thames'; but he places the name to poetic advantage, rhyming it with 'rock' and subordinating it to 'dead' with ominous precision.

There follows a temporary lull in the tragedy, as the night was succeeded by day and with day came a revival of hope; but the poet concentrates on the close of the lull, when 'Hope was twelve hours gone'. This is the hope which he again found in the newspaper reports of 11 December: 'The captain . . . had confident *hopes* of a speedy rescue. . . . Monday was a tolerably clear day; passing vessels were distinctly seen from the Deutschland's deck, and every effort was made to attract their attention. The passengers and crew watched those vessels, two of them steamers, *hoping* that each of them had seen, or must soon see, the signal of distress. But one after another passed by and night came on.' In his poetic treatment of these reports, just as he had personified Death in the opening stanza of this part, so he now personifies Hope as having grown old with 'grey hairs', and already in mourning as if for her own death. Then with a further exaggeration, recalling a line from Donne's *Twicknam Garden*, 'Blasted with sighs and surrounded with tears', he represents the face of Hope as 'Trenched with tears, carved with cares'. Finally, he speaks of her as 'twelve hours gone'—not in the sense of 'twelve hours ago' (in the normal understanding of the phrase), but of 'gone after twelve hours of expectation'. In 'hours' there is perhaps a foreshadowing of the word as emphasized in the dark sonnet *I wake and feel*: 'What hours, O what black hoürs we have spent', with the added explanation: 'But where I say / Hours, I mean years, mean life.'

In the next stanza the poet pauses to describe an incident reported in *The Times* of 11 December: 'One brave sailor, who was safe in the rigging, went down to try and save a child or woman who was drowning on deck. He was secured by a rope to the rigging, but a wave dashed him against the bulwarks.' In his narrative he again keeps close to the report, only varying his choice of words with an eye to their poetic effect within his metrical limits. Thus he chooses 'stirred' for its assonance with 'rigging' and alliteration with 'to save'; and he develops 'woman' into 'wild woman-kind'. He also draws a contrast between 'the wild woman-kind' in distress on deck and 'the man, handy and brave', who goes down to their rescue in a spirit of medieval chivalry. Above all, he draws the fundamental contrast between the utmost efforts of the man and the effortless power of Fate which frustrates him, with the simple statement: 'He was pitched to his death at a blow'. The effect of this statement is reinforced by its triple, anapaestic repetition of two un-stressed, followed by one stressed syllable: 'He was pítched | t͡ his déath | at blów.'

The poet now leads up to the grand climax on the following night, as a hopelessly unequal struggle is joined between the human mortals on board ship and the howling elements around them. Once again he derives his narrative from *The Times* report for 11 December: 'Most of the crew and many of the emigrants went into the rigging, where they were safe enough as long as they could maintain their hold. But the intense cold and long exposure told a tale. The purser of the ship, though a strong man, relaxed his grasp and fell into the sea. Women and children and men were one by one swept away from their shelters on the deck.' Improving on this account, he emphasizes the struggle with the verb 'fought', and he sees the cold not merely in its phenomenological aspect, but in its metaphysical relation to ultimate reality, as 'God's cold'. He also brings out the ruthless efficiency with which Fate overcomes its victims in their struggle—touching first on their general powerlessness: 'And they could not' (with an echo of the Quartermaster's words at an earlier stage in the story: 'We tried to get off, but could not'); then noting the particular effects one by one, as they 'fell to the deck', and it 'Crushed them', or into the 'water', and it 'drowned them', or else 'rolled / With the sea-romp over the wreck'. He presents everything as happening with swift compression of incident, as it were in the memory of the survivors who gave their reports to the newspapers, or rather in the vivid imagination of a ballad poet. To secure this effect, he has more than normal recourse to grammatical ellipsis, crushing words together no less ruthlessly than the deck crushed its victims as they fell. He then proceeds from a succession of ellipses to a more even flow of words, following 'the sea-romp over the wreck'. He presents everything as happening with swift compression of incident, as if it were some playful monster unaware of the suffering it is causing to mortal men. The crescendo comes with the opening words of the second half of the stanza: 'Night roared.'

Against this elaborate background of tragic incident, in a struggle to death between man and nature, Hopkins leads up to the main point of his poem. Out of the tumult of the storm is heard the 'one word necessary' uttered by the tall nun, as a prophetess with her 'virginal tongue'; and the corresponding effect on the poet is to 'make words break from me here all alone', as he recollects her emotion in the tranquillity of 'a pastoral forehead of Wales'. And so we are led back from the narrative of Part the Second to the main theme of his Pindaric Ode, which extends from the second to the first part, and from the first to the second half of each stanza—and from this chapter to the opening chapter of this book. Instead, therefore, of pursuing *The Wreck of the Deutschland* beyond the limits of a ballad, we may turn to the next example the poet affords of tragic narrative in *The Loss of the Eurydice* he composed some two years later.

15
Gone With the Gale

The Eurydice—it concerned thee, O Lord:
Three hundred souls, O alas! on board,
    Some asleep unawakened, all un-
warned, eleven fathoms fallen.

Where she foundered! One stroke
Felled and furled them, the hearts of oak!
    And flockbells off the aerial
Downs' forefalls beat to the burial.

For did she pride her, freighted fully, on
Bounden bales or a hoard of bullion?—
    Precious passing measure,
Lads and men her lade and treasure.

She had come from a cruise, training seamen—
Men, boldboys soon to be men:
    Must it, worst weather,
Blast bole and bloom together?

No Atlantic squall overwrought her
Or rearing billow of the Biscay water:
    Home was hard at hand
And the blow bore from land.

And you were a liar, O blue March day.
Bright sun lanced fire in the heavenly bay;
    But what black Boreas wrecked her? he
Came equipped, deadly-electric,

A beetling baldbright cloud thorough England
Riding: there did storms not mingle? and

The wreck of the 'Deutschland' as it appeared in the *Illustrated London News*
(18 December 1875)
Below The rescue of the survivors by a Harwich steam tug

HMS 'Eurydice' struck by a squall (*Illustrated London News*, 6 April 1878)
Below HMS 'Eurydice' as last seen by one of the survivors

Left Drawing of a tree by GMH, 1863
Right Drawing of hedgerow leaves and branches by GMH, 1863
Below right Drawing 'At the Baths of Rosenlaui' by GMH, 1868

GMH photographed with the community at Clongowes in 1884 or 1885
Below The inscription on the cross in the Jesuit plot at Glasnevin, Ireland

P. JOANNES CALLAN OBiiT MAii. 24 1888 ÆTAT. AN. 8

P. GERARDUS HOPKINS OBiiT JUN. 8 1889 ÆTAT. AN. 44
P. JACOBUS TUITE OBiiT NOV. 30 1891 ÆTAT. AN. 60
P. DANIEL SCULLY OBiiT JUN. 19 1892 ÆTAT. AN. 65
P. JACOBUS LYNCH OBiiT JAN. 1 1897 ÆTAT. AN. 43
P. JOANNES GAFFNEY OBiiT MAR. 31 1898 ÆTAT. AN. 84
P. ALFREDUS B. MURPHY OBiiT OCT 28 1902 ÆTAT. AN. 76
P. ROBERTUS CARBERY OBiiT SEP. 3 1903 ÆTAT. AN. 75

Hailropes hustle and grind their
Heavengravel? wolfsnow, worlds of it, wind there?

Now Carisbrook keep goes under in gloom;
Now it overvaults Appledurcombe;
   Now near by Ventnor town
It hurls, hurls off Boniface Down.

Too proud, too proud, what a press she bore!
Royal, and all her royals wore.
   Sharp with her, shorten sail!
Too late; lost; gone with the gale.

from *The Loss of the Eurydice*

At the time of composing this poem, Hopkins was no longer studying theology at St Beuno's College in North Wales, but more actively engaged in the less congenial task of bursar at the Jesuit boarding-school of Mount St Mary's in Derbyshire, amid what he calls 'the Sheffield smoke-ridden air'. In such circumstances he found his Muse had 'turned utterly sullen'; and it was only when he read the news of another shipwreck, the foundering of the Eurydice off the Isle of Wight on 24 March, 1878, that he felt the urge to compose another narrative poem. This time, in response to Bridges's criticism of his *Wreck of the Deutschland*, that it 'would be more generally interesting if there were more wreck and less discourse', he came out with a poem which he claimed was 'almost all narrative'. For this reason, however, its form is less clearly that of a ballad than what we find in the second part of *The Wreck of the Deutschland*, as the lyrical or meditative element is not separated from, but interfused with the narrative. Its rhythm is consequently more complex than that of the first half of the stanzas in *The Wreck*, and shows more use of what Hopkins calls 'my own rhythm', though (he adds) 'in a measure something like Tennyson's *Violet*'. Its movement is, moreover, slower and less allusive than that of Part the Second of *The Wreck*, as the poet tries out a variety of poetic effects, ranging from prayer, lament, rhetorical question, and factual statement, to personification and apostrophe, before coming at last to the tragic catastrophe in line 36: 'Too late; lost; gone with the gale.'

He opens with an emphasis on the ship's name, 'The Eurydice', in contrast to his almost off-handed way of mentioning it in his earlier poem: 'Into the snows she sweeps . . . The Deutschland, on Sunday'—as though adding it as an afterthought. Yet he does not pause to consider the significance of the name Eurydice, as he goes on to do in the earlier poem, in the parenthetical comment: 'O Deutschland, double a desperate name!' Instead, he seems to break off in uncontrollable emotion, and addresses his words directly to God—thereby collapsing together the elements of prayer and narration which he had kept apart in the other poem. He merely exclaims: 'It concerned thee, O Lord'; and there he leaves his prayer for the moment—having said enough to place the whole poem within the framework of colloquy—to resume it in his conclusion. He now goes on, as in Part the Second of *The Wreck*, to enumerate the 'souls' on board the ill-fated ship—this time 'three hundred' in the round. This time, too, the enumeration is not left as a mere fact, but accompanied by a subjective lament, 'O alas!'—in echo of Miranda's tender words at the beginning of *The Tempest*: 'Poor souls, they perish'd . . . O, woe the day!' Some of them, he reflects, were taken 'asleep unawakened'—possibly like Hamlet's father, even in the blossoms of their sin, and sent to their account with all their imperfections on their head. Now they lie, not 'full fathom five' like Ferdinand's father in Ariel's song, but 'eleven fathoms fallen'—with the theological implication of 'fallen', as unredeemed from original sin, like Henry Purcell 'listed to a heresy' and laid low at least by 'the outward sentence.'

Next, the poet reflects on the divine 'stroke' that 'Felled and furled them', not in a developing combination of unkind elements over a period of days as in the wreck of the Deutschland, but all at once 'in a crash' and a sudden squall of wind. Here, in a letter to Bridges written soon after from Stonyhurst on 30 May, 1878, he puts the rather literal-minded objection, 'How are hearts of oak furled?' and gives the answer: 'Well, in sound and sea water. . . . You are to suppose a stroke or blast in a forest of 'hearts of oak' . . . which at one blow both lays them low and buries them in broken earth.' He also points out that furling 'is proper when said of sticks and staves'. This suggests a connection of thought between the 'hearts of oak' and *Binsey Poplars*, where he laments how the trees are 'All felled, felled, are all felled', and then, more generally, how 'Strokes of havoc únselve / The sweet especial scene'. And there is his similar lament in *That Nature is a Heraclitean Fire*:

> Man, how fast his firedint, his mark on mind, is gone!
> Both are in an unfathomable, all is in an enormous dark
> Drowned.

At the same time, he notes a funeral significance, as of a 'passing bell', in the sound of the sheep's bells, or 'flockbells', carried by the wind 'off the aerial / Downs' forefalls'. Directly, these words refer to the lofty downs of the Isle of Wight as they fall steeply down to the foreshore; but in 'aerial' there is also the suggestion of something heavenly, like the mysterious sound of the 'Blue-beating and hoary-glow height' and the 'night, still higher, / With belled fire' of *The Wreck* stanza 26. The possibility is also suggested that these heavenly bells serve, like the 'breast of the / Maiden' in *The Wreck* stanza 31, to 'Startle the poor sheep back' to God, thereby transforming the shipwreck into a harvest and the tempest into a conveyor of grain to heaven.

Then there follows a question and answer. Did the ship pride herself on a full freight of bales of merchandise, or gold bullion, and so incurred her just fall? Had she not after all just come from the fabled land of El Dorado in the Spanish Main? No, the poet answers; but she could boast of a load and a treasure of far greater worth. For hers was a load and treasure of 'Lads and men' returning from a training cruise in the West Indies. Such a load, he adds, is indeed 'Precious passing measure', like that he indicates in *The Wreck* stanza 26: 'What by your measure is the heaven of desire, / The treasure never eyesight got, nor was ever guessed what for the hearing.' This reference to 'Lads and men' naturally leads, in the next stanza, to a fuller description of the former as 'boldboys soon to be men'. They are seen in the attractive bloom of youth, when 'the heart rears wings bold and bolder'; and they have just returned 'from a cruise, training seamen', a calling which Hopkins particularly admired as manly. It is this which makes their tragedy all the more lamentable; and so, anticipating what is yet to come in his narrative, he plaintively questions: 'Must it, worst weather, / Blast bole and bloom together?' In terms of these 'hearts of oak', he thinks of the men among them as the 'bole' of the tree, and the boys as the 'bloom'—or, as he says elsewhere, 'Breathing bloom of a chastity in mansex fine', in the time of their 'innocent mind and Mayday'.

But now, at the very end of their cruise, when 'Home was hard at hand', and the blow all the harder to bear, the ship was struck by a cruel Fate (or a kind Providence?). What 'overwrought her', the poet notes with poignant regret, was not a gale such as might have been anticipated in the Atlantic, nor a rough sea with 'rearing billow' such as might well have been encountered in the Bay of Biscay, but a blow that bore down on them all the more unexpectedly as it came from home, from the English mainland—after they had come safely through all foreign dangers. The enumeration of these possibilities, in contrast to the actual event, serves only to slow down the pace of the poem. And this is also the effect of the apostrophe which follows, as the poet turns to address the 'blue March day' that begot the 'black Boreas' that wrecked the ship.

Conceiving the day thus as a person, he accuses her of being 'a liar', for her fair appearance hiding so foul a catastrophe about to befall them. Outwardly, all seemed fair, as the 'Bright sun lanced fire in the heavenly bay'—in what is presented in *The Wreck* stanza 12 as the bay of God's blessing, vaulting in all humanity. But the lance of disaster was flung, not by the sun from above, but by a cold wind from the North, equipped as it was with deadly electricity or 'electrical horror'.

As he now proceeds to follow the path of this 'beetling baldright cloud thorough England'—with a suggestion of Yorkshire in the participle 'Riding'—the poet himself begins to gather an answering speed and to accelerate the pace of his poem into something more like a ballad. In his description the cloud, menacingly overhanging like 'cliffs of fall', while bright in its outer and upper portions like the bald head of a man, comes with bold velocity—mingling storms in its troubled centre, hustling hail like rope together, and grinding a heavenly kind of gravel. Also with its hailstones it has wound worlds of snow like wool on cards, packing it together like 'wiry and white-fiery' wolves on a raid in a wintry forest. This is all phrased in a series of questions, coming thick and fast, like the hailropes and wolfsnow in the storms that mingle in the cloud. But now, with the approach of the cloud to the South Coast, another series of affirmations follows, as the poet refers to different localities on the Isle of Wight that might stand up as landmarks for the seamen of the Eurydice. First, the keep of Carisbrooke Castle 'goes under in gloom', as it were prophetic of what is to befall the ship. Then the crest of Appledurcombe, with its farm and manor-house, is vaulted over by the blast. Finally, from above the seaside town of Ventnor, the gale hurls with unleashed ferocity off the brow of Boniface Down and sweeps down on to the Channel and the ship.

Coming now to his catastrophe, the poet watches the impact of this sudden squall on the ship. He laments her splendid appearance, 'with all sail set' (as the reports described her) making for harbour; but it was 'Too proud, too proud'. He remarks on 'what a press she bore'—in both senses of pressing on to harbour, and bearing a fine complement or press of men on board. There is even something royal or majestic about her, wearing as she does even her royal sails up to the tops of her masts, as stately robes in a solemn procession. But interrupting himself, he calls on her to look sharp and 'shorten sail', before the storm hits her. Yet even as he speaks, it is 'too late': the storm has hit her, and all is 'lost'. Suddenly, even in an instant, she has 'gone with the gale'. Already the gale has passed, the sun is shining again; but there is no sign of the ship.

Such a climax, told with a striking economy of words, is in the best ballad tradition; but as the moment passes, the manner of the poet also passes. He goes on to describe how Death came 'teeming in by her portholes', and how the men found themselves unable to escape from the ship which 'Was around them, bound them or wound them with her'. He presents the various fates of Marcus Hare, the captain, who goes down with his charge; of 'Sydney Fletcher, Bristol-bred', who is one of the only two survivors; of 'one sea-corpse cold', who is 'all of lovely manly mould', yet 'one like thousands more'. But he is no longer primarily interested in his narrative. He is looking beyond these individual tragedies, and the collective tragedy of the Eurydice, to the larger one reflected in them on a smaller scale, the tragedy of his own 'people and born own nation, / Fast foundering own generation'. In the drowned sailors of the Eurydice, as in the 'comfortless unconfessed' of the passengers and crew of the Deutschland, it is for England he laments: for the 'hoar-hallowèd shrines unvisited' of Canterbury and Walsingham and Holywell, and still more for the 'breathing' temples of men rolled, like these sailors, in ruin. Thus his incipient ballad turns, not like *The Wreck of the Deutschland* into a Pindaric Ode, but into a Theocritean Elegy. It is an Elegy that is not just a lament for the unredeemable past, but also a prayer for the future that yet retains hope and promise. And it is in this hope that he turns his attention—in a movement strikingly similar to that of *The Wreck*—from the earthly years of mother and wife and sweetheart to the figure of Christ as 'lord of thunder'. He it is who makes use of 'wrecking and storm' to wring the rebellious wills of men, and so to redeem 'souls sunk in seeming'. At the same time, it is the ever fresh prayer of his servants on earth that wins for their fellow-men the 'pity eternal' which reprieves them from 'doomfire', or 'world's wildfire', and reveals them—now shorn of all triviality—as 'immortal diamond'.

16
Where Storms Not Come

A nun takes the veil

I have desired to go
    Where springs not fail,
To fields where flies no sharp and sided hail
    And a few lilies blow.

And I have asked to be
    Where no storms come,
Where the green swell is in the havens dumb,
    And out of the swing of the sea.

Heaven–Haven

Here, in one of his earliest and best loved poems, Hopkins gives expression—in the person of a nun about to take the veil—to a deep desire for peace and rest after the struggles of life in this world. To some this desire may seem uncharacteristic of the dynamic energy which fills the poems of his maturity and inspires him with delight when he finds a similar energy outside himself—in *The Windhover*, for instance. It is precisely out of the struggles of life—such as he describes in *The Wreck of the Deutschland* (stanza 2): 'And the midriff astrain with leaning of, laced with fire of stress', that he comes to experience the stroke and the stress 'that stars and storms deliver' (stanza 6). So it would seem that for him, where there is no more struggle, there can be no more life. Then Death supervenes, to blot 'manshape' black out. All the same, through all his poems, even or especially in those of his maturity, there runs an unmistakable contrapuntal theme of craving for peace—such peace as he briefly enjoyed during his last year or two of theological studies at St Beuno's.

Thus at the heart of *The Wreck of the Deutschland* there is at least the suggestion, possibly recalled from *Heaven-Haven*, that the nun is calling on Christ in the storm in order 'The keener to come at the comfort for feeling the combating keen'. It is true that the poet goes on to turn down this suggestion; but he recognizes it as 'What by your measure is the heaven of desire, / The treasure never eyesight got, nor was ever guessed what for the hearing'. The suggestion may not perhaps apply to the nun amid her 'danger, electrical horror'; but it may well apply to the poet himself, sheltered as he is 'under a roof here' and at rest 'On a pastoral forehead of Wales'. For it is precisely, he affirms, 'the jading and jar of the cart, / Time's tasking,' which 'fathers that asking for ease / Of the sodden-with-its-sorrowing heart'.

This is a feeling which Hopkins had already experienced more than once in the course of his long studies as a Jesuit—and not least in the years immediately preceding his composition of *The Wreck*. Thus in 1873 we find a record in his Journal of how he felt unwell and downcast, when it seemed to him 'nature in all her parcels and faculties gaped and fell apart, *fatiscebat*, like a clod cleaving and holding only by strings of root'. There follows the significant addition: 'But this must often be.' Again in 1874 we find him complaining of being tired and cast down, with the more general comment: 'Altogether perhaps my heart has never been so burdened and cast down as this year.' It is not unlikely that this period of ill-health was in his memory when he wrote in the first stanza of *The Wreck*: 'And after it almost unmade, what with dread, / Thy doing.' Then out of the depth of this despondency he felt the finger of God touching him afresh on the occasion of a shipwreck and raising him to new heights of poetic inspiration—as he found his own petty cares drowned in the greater physical sufferings of those on board the Deutschland.

This springtime of his religious life and poetry did not, however, last for long. We soon find the poet relapsing into his old confessions of ill-health and frustration, and expressing his corresponding desires for peace and rest. This feeling is concentrated in a curtal sonnet he composed during his stay at St Aloysius's, Oxford, with the significant title of *Peace*. The object of his desire he personifies in the form of a 'wild wooddove' who is ever roaming round him, but never settling 'shy wings shut' under his boughs. Such peace as (he admits) he enjoys from time to time is but a 'piecemeal peace'; and in lieu of his ideal he must needs put up with Patience that 'plumes to Peace thereafter'. The more experience he has of pastoral work as a priest, the stronger grows his temptation to fall into Despair and Carrion Comfort. Momentarily he may hear the invitation of the Golden Echo to resign himself and to follow 'yonder'; but for the most part it seems as if he is more conscious of the seductive Leaden Echo, directing his steps steadily downwards from the bright to the dark poems.

The depth of darkness is plumbed in the sonnet *No worst, there is none,* where the poet looks in vain for such shelter as may serve 'in a whirlwind'. The only comfort he can find is in the apparent despair of his concluding reflection: 'all / Life death does end and each day dies with sleep.' In his Irish exile the day brings him no respite from his weariness of 'idle a being but by where wars are rife'. But even at night he can find no rest, as he lies awake ever tormenting his tormented mind with his tormented mind. He cannot get away from his suffering, any more than he can get away from himself; for

God's most deep decree
Bitter would have me taste: my taste was me.

More than ever before he comes to feel that his present need is not just for Peace, but for Patience. Yet what he most needs he finds hardest to pray for; since 'Patience who asks / Wants war, wants wounds; weary his times, his tasks.' In *The Wreck* he had already recorded this experience of 'Time's tasking'; but now he is more feelingly persuaded of what he is, and what he needs.

What he needs above all is 'comfort', a word that recurs in a variety of ways in his poems of this period. The reality comes at last when he leaves it 'root-room', when he looks from his tormented mind to the Heraclitean fire of nature around him. There he finds everything in a state of perpetual flux, rising upwards to air and fire, falling downwards to water and earth. There the tempest of yesterday is succeeded by today's 'bright wind boisterous' which 'ropes, wrestles, beats earth bare'. In this consideration he finds something at first refreshing and invigorating. Yet in its continuation he feels himself drawn into a deeper despair, at the contrast between the irrepressible resurgence of 'Million-fuelèd, nature's bonfire' and the stark disappearance of 'her clearest-selvèd spark / Man'. In his case, it seems, 'all is in an enormous dark / Drowned' and lost forever. But that is only as it seems. Now as swiftly as the bright winds have cleared away 'yestertempest's creases', so his faith in the Resurrection clears away his despair, and restores hope to his mind. Significantly, he recurs to the imagery of *The Wreck*: 'Across my foundering deck shone / A beacon, an eternal beam.' It is, he realizes, only mortal flesh which fades and falls 'to the residuary worm', or becomes fuel for 'world's wildfire'. As for himself, in his immortal spirit, his eyes are opened to see how

> In a flash, at a trumpet crash,
> I am all at once what Christ is, since he was what I am.

Then from the insignificance of his earthly life he rears himself and is revealed in heavenly splendour as 'immortal diamond'.

It is only in one respect, therefore, that the journey, or rather the pilgrimage, of his earthly life may be said to have its end in the little Jesuit plot situated in a corner of the cemetery of Glasnevin in Dublin. Here rest his mortal remains, with those of other Irish Jesuit fathers and brothers, at the foot of a great granite crucifix, with his name inscribed not individually over his grave but communally beneath the crucifix. Thus he maintained up to the end that anonymity of community life which was his lot on earth as a member of the Society of Jesus. His own individual monument to posterity, signed with his own name, was not unveiled till many years later, when his friend Robert Bridges edited the first edition of his poems in 1918—thereby ensuring that his 'eternal summer' would not fade, but that in his 'eternal lines' he would grow to time. His death in 1889 was followed (so to say) by the silence of an 'aposiopesis'; but this in turn has been followed by the glory of 'apotheosis', both inwardly in the minds of admiring readers, and outwardly in the stained-glass window depicting him in the parish church of Haslemere.

Now his devotees are following in his footsteps to Glasnevin, not just as the final resting-place of a famous poet, but even as the shrine of a saint, whose poetry points the way not only 'from heaven to earth', but also 'from earth to heaven'. So it was that in the summer of 1972, on the occasion of a literary and historical pilgrimage through the British Isles, I brought a group of Japanese teachers and students, including not a few members of the Hopkins Society of Japan, to Dublin and to the cemetery of Glasnevin. There before the Jesuit plot and the granite crucifix we stood in silent prayer, not for Hopkins, as for one in need, but to Hopkins, as to a saint in heaven. Such was the prayer he himself prays in his poems, not only to God, but also to Mary and his saints—including the 'Dame, at our door / Drowned': that 'for souls sunk in seeming' the power of his words may 'fetch pity eternal' and bring them—'never ask if meaning it, wanting it, warned of it—to hero of Calvary, Christ's feet', and so to 'the heaven-haven of the reward'.

This is the ultimate tendency of all Hopkins's work on earth, both as a priest and as a poet. In the minds of his critics these two vocations often seem to come into conflict, if not into collision; but in his own mind they came together in perfect harmony, at least in their conclusion. To separate the one from the other is to do a serious injustice to the one as to the other. The poetry of Hopkins is at once that of a poet and that of a priest; and in its inmost essence, even while it celebrates the joys of the natural world and the sorrows of the inner world of man, it looks beyond both to the glories of the higher, supernatural world of God.

Appendix

Gerard Manley Hopkins: Dates, Places and Poems

1844   Born at Stratford, in Essex (*28 July*).

1852   Family moves to Oak Hill, Hampstead, London.

1854   Enters Highgate School, London.
Spends several summer holidays in Shanklin in the Isle of Wight.

1863   Enters Oxford University, Balliol College.
   Heaven–Haven, May 1866.

1866   Received into the Catholic Church by Newman at the Oratory, Birmingham (*21 Oct*).

1867   Classics master at Oratory School, Birmingham.

1868   Enters Jesuit noviciate at Manresa House, Roehampton (*7 Sept*).

1870   Begins study of scholastic philosophy at St Mary's Hall, Stonyhurst, Lancs. (*9 Sept*).

1873   Returns to Roehampton to teach Classics to Jesuit 'juniors' (*29 Aug*).

1874   Begins study of theology at St Beuno's College in North Wales, in the Vale of Clwyd (*28 Aug*).
   The Wreck of the Deutschland, early 1876;
   God's Grandeur, Feb 1877;
   In the Valley of the Elwy, May 1877;
   The Windhover, May 1877;
   Pied Beauty, Summer 1877;
   Hurrahing in Harvest, Sept 1877.

1877   Ordained priest at St Beuno's (*23 Sept*).
Sub-minister (bursar) at Mount St Mary's College in Derbyshire (*19 Oct*).
   The Loss of the Eurydice, April 1878.

1878   Coaching boys in Classics at Stonyhurst College in Lancashire (*April*).
    The May Magnificat, May 1878.
Preacher at Farm Street Church, London (*July*).
On the staff of St Aloysius's Church, Oxford (*Dec*).
    Binsey Poplars, March 1879.

1879   On the staff of St Joseph's Church, Leigh in Lancashire (*Oct*).
    Began *St Winefred's Well*, Oct 1879.
On the staff of St Francis Xavier's Church, Liverpool (*Dec*), (where he preached many of his best sermons).
    Spring and Fall, Sept 1880.

1881   On supply at St Joseph's Church, Glasgow (*10 Aug*).
    Inversnaid, Sept 1881.
Begins tertianship at Manresa House, Roehampton (where he wrote his Commentary on the *Spiritual Exercises*) (*8 Oct*).

1882   Classics master at Stonyhurst College (*22 Aug*).
    Ribblesdale, 1882.

1884   Professor of Classics at University College, Dublin, Royal University of Ireland (*Feb*).
    Spelt from Sibyl's Leaves, early 1885;
    Completed *St Winefred's Well*, April 1885;
    On the Portrait, Dec 1886;
    That Nature is a Heraclitean Fire, July 1888.

1889   Died of typhoid fever in Dublin; buried in the Jesuit plot at Glasnevin Cemetery (*8 June*).

Index